No Perfect Fathers Here

By CHRIS SPICER

No Perfect Fathers Here

ISBN-10: 1-451553-30-7

EAN-13: 978-1-451553-30-7

Copyright © 2010 by Chris Spicer

www.chrisspicer.net

Published by

CHRIS SPICER

Cover design & character illustration by **Design Jones Ltd** (www.designjones.co.uk)

Dedicated to four wonderful children
who dare to call me Dad.

Acknowledgements

That this book ever found its way to the publishers is thanks to a number of wonderful people.

In the first place I must say a big thank you to my heavenly Father, for He alone is the Perfect Father, whose parenting example portrayed in the Scriptures is the foundation on which this book is built. Secondly, a big thank you to four wonderful people who, by calling me Dad, have allowed me the opportunity to experience, and at times experiment in, the role and responsibility of fatherhood. Thanks also to their mother and my wife, Tina, who time and time again has had to make up for my deficiency in the realm of parenting and without whose friendship and encouragement this book would never have made it to the printers.

To my biological father and the numerous spiritual fathers whose mentoring moments have taught me what it means to be a better dad, I simply say, "Thanks guys." And then finally thanks to my son Luther for producing all the wonderful graphics, my daughter Hannah for internal layout, Martha Mackey for the hours she volunteered to proofread the text and Nancy Kanafani whose editorial expertise made sense of my scribbling and made the unreadable readable.

Chris Spicer

Chris Spicer takes on one of the most pressing issues of our time, father-less-ness. Through thoughtful and creative angles he shows us what it looks like when the heart of a father turns toward his children. As a father of four young children, I treasure the seasoned wisdom offered here.

J.D. Walt, Dean of the Chapel, Asbury Theological Seminary

What an incredible resource for fathers, 'would be' fathers, and those feeling imperfect as fathers. The honesty and vulnerability, together with wonderful illustrations, make this a must read for those of us who know this stuff doesn't always come naturally. My experience in reading 'No Perfect Fathers Here' is made deeper by the fact of knowing the author, both as a friend and colleague in the work of God for thirty-plus years. The book comes from a heart passionate to see godly fathers raised up in this generation. No one serious about this God-given calling to be fathers should miss the opportunity of reading it.

John King, Senior Pastor, Riverside Community Church

What a refreshing title, "NO PERFECT FATHERS HERE!" This book brings a smile to my face and a big AMEN to my lips. A great read for all fathers who sometimes feel like a failure.

Greg Vaughn, Author/Founder *Letters from Dad*

Medicine can be made "child proof." But children can't be made "parent proof." Chris Spicer has written a masterful book on male parenting from which even the best-placed or worst-qualified parent can draw wisdom of the heart, mind, and body.

Leonard Sweet, best-selling author of *The Gospel According to Starbucks, So Beautiful,* and *The Jesus Manifesto*

It's been said that today's generation of young people - those in the 14-35 age bracket - are the generation of divorced parents, absent fathers and broken homes. More than any other in history, this generation is the fatherless generation. *No Perfect Fathers Here* seeks to address the problem and is a book I'd highly recommend for all fathers to prayerfully read.

Mark Stibbe, author of *The Father You've Been Waiting For*

Chris is a faithful and insightful leader. He has a great grasp on what it means to be a Godly father, a Christ-like father, and a father equipped by God with special grace to be the best father you can be. Enjoy, and make this book a prayerful read.

Dr. Frank Damazio,
Lead Pastor,
City Bible Church

"No Perfect Fathers Here" is for every father who knows the frustration of having a desire to be a great father but has very little direction on how to achieve it. Chris Spicer masterfully blends personal candor, biblical truth and practical insight to encourage and challenge "imperfect fathers," like me, to embrace our God given calling and privilege. This book is a must read for every father who desires healing and help.

Deveraux R. Hubbard, Senior Pastor, St Paul's Baptist Church

I'm often reminded that I'm not a perfect dad; my son even scored me "average" on one of our fathering profiles. When I share that story with men, I always sense a sigh of relief from them, and that's one of the many strengths of Chris Spicer's book. There's no pressure to be the perfect dad, but he explores many vital roles of fatherhood and equips every dad to be the unique father God has called him to be. This is a great read for anyone serious about the role and responsibility of fathering.

Carey Casey, CEO National Center for Fathering / fathers.com, author of *Championship Fathering*

Foreword

When I first became a father on March 10, 1988, my wife and I were both on the cusp of our 27th birthdays. Following a picture perfect pregnancy with excellent pre-natal care, we both eagerly anticipated the birth of our first child, Patrick Henry Hughes. But he came into this world not at all as I expected.

Our son had "multiple anomalies": bi-lateral anophthalmia—his eyes just didn't develop; he had Pterygia Syndrome— his arms and legs were constricted at his elbows and knees, respectively. And more tests and time would determine what else might be wrong with our baby.

The first few weeks of Patrick's life we spent crying ourselves to sleep, asking why us? What did we do wrong? Did God find disfavor with me? Was my arrogance and attitude something that needed to be adjusted quickly in order for me to be a better father to my children? The questions we asked at this time eventually ran the gamut of emotions—sorrow, anger, rage, denial, and soon enough, acceptance. My wife and I began to ask, "Why not us?"

As Patrick's father, once the acceptance of his differences took hold, I became like most other new dads. I didn't have all the answers, but I loved and enjoyed him, regularly told him so and showed him so with my words and time (as I did with my other two sons; all three are becoming fine young men). I also fell many times and made a lot of mistakes.

I didn't have a roadmap to follow as I started out on my journey as a dad, so I struggled greatly for many years. That's why I so appreciate Chris Spicer's wonderful compilation of 10 attributes of what a father can be. Looking back I've attempted, with various degrees of success, to be all ten of the characteristics outlined in his book with my three children. Yet, perhaps the *Composer Father* is the one characteristic that resonates most with my story. As someone who loves music I've tried to appreciate the unique song in each of my sons, and give them sufficient individual space to contribute to that glorious symphony we call life. In reading through this message you may be surprised to find one or more characteristics resonating with you as well.

I recommend that all dads consider *No Perfect Fathers Here* as they raise their children. It promises to be an essential guidebook to those guys who find themselves journeying on the ups and downs of the road we call Fatherhood. While your struggles and successes may not be the same as mine, the principles found in these pages will prove to be a source of great encouragement to imperfect fathers the world over.

Patrick John Hughes

Contents

INTRODUCTION

I'm a father. Biologically I have played my part in producing four great kids. But looking back at my meager efforts at playing the role of a dad, I have to admit that my numerous theories all got mugged along the way by the practical realities of having children. Fatherhood is a practice learned on the job and while few of us have any previous experience in this area, many of us try to do the best we can in a role for which we often feel totally unqualified.

So, let's make it abundantly clear: this is not a book written by an expert for trainees. If you want those books, you'd be well advised to keep searching. You'll find out in this one that there's no such thing as a perfect father — only real dads who often struggle with their short-comings and failings, who know both the sweet scent of success and the horrid stench of failure.

You may be reeling from your own well-documented fathering imperfections. But no matter how good or bad you might feel about yourself as a dad, this message is intended to be a source of relief for you and hope for more successful days ahead. *For none of us can afford to allow our mistakes and sometimes feeble attempts at fathering to take us out of the most crucial game of life – parenting.*

Numerous times as a Christian minister I have seen firsthand the sad state of affairs in society nowadays: most men are well able to produce offspring, yet an increasing number of dads seem incapable of building character in or mentoring their own kids towards their God-given destiny. It could be due to growing up with poor father role-models or no father role-models at all, as the "experts" love to debate. In a world of hurt where society seems to take pleasure in bashing dads, I won't be debating or discussing these negative aspects. Rather, I embrace the positive side and approach fatherhood using a two-fold "line of attack."

I've written about the lives of some extraordinary people, so you could describe *No Perfect Fathers Here* as more storybook than textbook. A collection of snapshots and stories taken from real life, it also brings together a number of key concepts that characterize what real fathering is all about. I've built this book around ten traits that portray ten particular aspects of male parenting. You won't find any major or minor players in these. Every colorfully different character brings to the stage a unique caricature of present-day fatherhood that is buttressed by individual and group discussion questions for personal introspection and reflection.

Collectively, they create a kind of parental sketchbook that offers help and encouragement to those of us who are employed in the most influential job in the whole world, while coaching us in some classic life lessons crucial for anyone who wants to be an effective dad.

It is my hope that this message will clarify the difference between *becoming* a father and *being* a father. That is a prominent theme that threads its way throughout the book and is built on the fundamental foundation that it takes the grace of God to *be* a dad. God's grace isn't something mysterious. Simply put, it's strength, wisdom and help from God to enable us to do what we can't do on our own—meaning we're not in this thing alone.[1] Knowing that should make all of us feel so much better!

And there's one more thing you should know before you begin.

Skimmer, Swimmer or Soaker?
Researchers reckon that the average 18-to 34-year-old red-blooded male would rather spend 22 hours a week surfing the Internet than read a book, watch television or make love to his wife. This naturally leads to the conclusion that *dudes don't read.* Therefore, if you have made it to this page, you deserve to be congratulated: *Well done, you've bucked the trend!*

To be bold enough to dive into any book is one thing, but to test the waters of an unknown author is something else. So whether you jumped or were pushed, your approach to reading this one will in all probability be similar to the way boys mess around with water: your reading style will either be that of a *skimmer, swimmer* or *soaker.*

Skimmers, like their stone-bouncing counterparts, don't want to experience the water for themselves. They merely see it as a means to get the biggest "bounce for their buck." As they skim through the literary pages, their goal is to achieve the maximum amount of knowledge for the minimum amount of effort. Gaining little long-term effect on their lives, they skip-read each chapter with one thing in mind — *content.* So, if you're a *skimmer,* you've already nailed the title, noted the content and concluded whether or not this book is going to be of any further use to you.

Swimmers, on the other hand, are not into a book for its mere contents; they're into it for *fun.* If the book looks inviting, they dive straight in without a moment's hesitation. And while preferring a more freestyle approach to reading, *swimmers* have a tendency to skip-read a book in order to submerge themselves into those chapters they believe offer the greatest thrill. Occasionally coming up for air, *swimmers* will stay in a book only as long as it fills a void between their other more important activities. So whereas *skimmers* peruse a book for their own ego, *swimmers* dive in for enjoyment.

Soakers, however, dare to be different. More subdued and contemplative in their approach, they mull over and marinate in a book's contents, while at the same time enjoying the whole reading experience. Soakers' sole purpose in submerging themselves into any literary enterprise is to discover *a life-changing thought*. With mandatory pen in hand, they set out on a new reading expedition, fully expecting to be challenged by a "eureka moment" — some mind-blowing, earth-shattering, life-changing revelation that affects the way they do life. Prepared to underline a key passage or doodle in the margin, they'll do whatever it takes to maximize the experience, which makes any book previously owned by a *soaker* something personal and precious.

Realizing that *skimmers* have long since left the building and *swimmers* have already dipped in and out of this literary pool, my preference is *soakers* — guys who will give quality time to marinate in the message. Regardless of your reading style, however, I urge you to soak long enough in the content to secure at least one life-changing thought.

Whether you have been given this book or you actually purchased it, I believe that you will find its contents useful. As a celebration of fatherhood, it is designed to encourage, equip and enable you to play your part in what is unquestionably one of the most significant jobs any man will undertake in his lifetime. May it become to you something of a road map to better parenting for that brief journey of life we get to enjoy with our children. I know for a fact how short that journey is, for my four children are all grown up now. Yet being their dad didn't end when they turned eighteen.

Just like the parable Jesus told of a man accidently finding treasure hidden in a field for years,[2] some of the things outlined here are things which I have stumbled on by accident, while others I have searched for over an almost forty year journey of being a father. Confession, they say, is good for the soul. If that is true, then this book is about to improve my health no end!

While others strive for perfection, I have come to realize two things: To arrive at a point at which we could not be bettered is an illusionary myth. To become everything God intended us to be as fathers is a real possibility. I hope to make that possibility a reality for you.

No Perfect Fathers Here

Screenwriter William Goldman has said that, in spite of all the experience that Hollywood people have in making movies, "Nobody knows anything." I sometimes think the same thing is true of raising children.

Bill Cosby[1]

Determining to Be a Dad
Who Makes the Difference

Dr. Huxtable, played by well-known comedian Bill Cosby in the 1980s sitcom *The Cosby Show*, seemed to be the epitome of fatherhood. With each episode came a crisis, conflict and celebration that the inimitable doctor handled effortlessly with the ease and expertise of a near-perfect parent—all while pursuing a successful career. When it comes to fatherhood, few of us measure up to the picture of perfection presented by a number of media role-models.

As a young father who grew up watching *Little House on the Prairie*, *The Waltons* and *The Cosby Show*, such family programming only served to feed my own feelings of personal inadequacy as a dad. My feeble attempts to be a good father of four young children fell far short of what these guys were portraying in their roles as fathers.

How many of us can look back over our own career as a dad and conclude that we have been "practically perfect in every way" (the term used to define the infamous surrogate parent Mary

Poppins in Disney's movie *Mary Poppins*)? I'm just guessing, but if you're anything like me, those are not quite the words you'd use to define your own role as a father.

The fact is there's no such person as a perfect father, save God our heavenly Father—and He has some rebellious sons with whom He strives daily to bring back to the straight and narrow way of living a God-fearing life. Perfect or not, there is perhaps no greater long-lasting influence on a young child than that of his or her parents, and with that duo the positive affect of a good father is inescapable. Research is conclusive that the male role-model is important in the social, mental, moral and spiritual development of a child.

A dad's role has significantly changed over the years—the hunter-gatherer that fought off tribal attacks has, in most cultures, been relegated to the history books. Although some fathers struggle with their newfound responsibilities, the world is waking up to the fact that the involvement of a positive male role model in the home is crucial, not only for each child, but for the world as a whole. If we're to stop the unraveling fabric of our society, fathers have to play their part.

Applauding his own father's positive influence on his life, Martin Luther King, Jr. once wrote, "The thing that I admire most about my dad is his genuine Christian character. He is a man of real integrity, deeply committed to moral and ethical principles. He is conscientious in all of his undertakings. Even the person who disagrees with his frankness has to admit that his motives and actions are sincere."[2] If only all children could express the same level of admiration for their fathers, perhaps society would not be facing some of its present challenges: for starters, the lack of strong fathers in the home is linked to higher rates of poverty, failure in school, teen pregnancy, substance abuse, violent crime and depression.

The modern man is fast losing the paper reading, lawn mowing and trash removing image that has for so long caricatured the Western culture's view of fatherhood. The distressing facts speak for themselves, but if humanity persists in weakening the biblical view of a husband and wife raising those children placed in their charge, then the future outcome on humanity will be catastrophic. Recent studies into the behavior of rogue elephants are a vivid reminder of this.

Young aggressive elephants had been uncharacteristically killing rhinos in a number of South African game parks. Orphaned when their parents were culled in the early 1990s, these animals had developed serious teenage temper tantrums. Some rangers who had witnessed these random acts of hooliganism spoke of how young elephants would uncharacteristically knock over a rhino and trample it under foot before driving a tusk into the victim's chest. In an effort to resolve this problem, it was decided to introduce a number of adult bull elephants into the parks. Amazingly, the rangers discovered that the influence of having a few adult males around was enough to stop the killing and bring these traumatized "teenagers" back into line.

All of which leads me to believe one thing: *the kind of world we want our grandchildren to enjoy tomorrow depends on the kind of fathering we engage in today.*

But perhaps we are getting ahead of ourselves. Before we discuss the *purpose* of fatherhood, we ought to define the *person*.

What Is a Father?

As a sixty-two-year-old granddad and Englishman living in America, I was born when a *Big Mac* was an oversized raincoat; a *chip* was a fried potato; *hardware* meant nuts and bolts; *software* wasn't a word; *pot* was a cooking utensil; a *joint* was a piece of meat; and to be *gay* had a totally different connotation. So to avoid any confusion, we should have common agreement on what exactly we mean by the term *father* before we continue.

One dictionary I consulted defined *father* as "a male parent...an important figure in the origin and early history of something...a male ancestor..." and "(in Christian belief) the first person of the Trinity; God."[3] Other dictionaries add such phrases as "a man who has begotten a child"[4] or "he who creates, invents, makes or composes any thing,"[5] "a person who founds a line or family" and "to be the biological cause of the conception and birth of a child."[6] While their conclusions may be correct, their definitions are devoid of depth, responsibly shallow, morally weak, and seemingly rather cold, calculated and somewhat clinical.

To simply define a male parent as a biological beginner of things is to me an insult to the role and responsibility of fatherhood. A founder, yes; but what of the future development of that which he has enabled to be formed in the female womb? Surely the essence of true fatherhood is more than the contribution of an infinitesimal measurement of sperm—what of the sacrificial commitment to what he has in turn helped to create? For surely the destiny of the one is wrapped up in the destiny of the other. Does a scientist birth a discovery only to ignore its potential? Does an athlete tirelessly prepare for a race only to quit in the starting blocks? Does an entrepreneur begin a company only to announce its formation and forgo any future investment?

We accredit Alexander Fleming with the discovery of penicillin, but had not Howard Walter Florey further developed the full potential of this antibiotic, the casualties of World War II might have been doubled. Historians have always associated the creation of the incandescent electric light with Thomas Edison, when in reality he only furthered the work of Humphrey Davy's "arc lamp." And while the Wright brothers are often attributed with the invention of flight, they simply developed a concept already known. So to define fathers as mere founders with little or no responsibility to invest in the future of what they have in part created is a travesty of the truth. The fact is, a moment of passion has the potential to result in a lifetime obligation

God's Best Gift

Any mature, healthy male can biologically *become* a father; it takes care, courage, consistency and commitment to *be* a father. For instance, you may have chosen to trade in your two-seater sports car for an SUV and enough hand luggage to equip an expedition to the Himalayas. You've volunteered to give up the quiet nights and tranquil moments of adult conversation for the bedlam of bath, bottle and bedtime. You've made a calculated choice to turn your furniture over to a tribe of trampoline and trapeze artists who have no idea how much that sofa is worth from which they are about to take one giant leap for mankind.

Whatever the reasons, you have decided to have children, or as Bill Cosby so aptly put it, "I guess the real reason that my wife and I had children is the same reason Napoleon had for invading Russia: it seemed like a good idea at the time."[7] So either by desire or default, you now find yourself caring for one or more children. You have to face the fact that you're now a father and, unlike most new appliances, babies don't come with instruction manuals.

Shattering our silence and rearranging the home, children burst onto the scene like a human wrecking ball demolishing our sanity, sense of well-being, and a pristine piece of real estate we call *home*. While thoughts of our own fathers' failings might clarify the fact that we at least are determined not to repeat history and make the same mistakes they did, the rest is uncertain. Theories get mugged by reality, and in no time we are awakened to the truth that we are now responsible for a screaming bundle of joy that has taken over the nest and caused us to lose things at an alarming rate — sleep, silence, space and, at times, our own sanity as evidenced by our darkened eyes, tired limbs, wrecked homes and depleted bank balances.

These snapshots of life can only mean one thing: a baby has arrived and your world has been turned upside down as the initial euphoria of new life gives way to the realities of parenthood. With a smile big enough to take in the western hemisphere, the rest of the world may be left in no doubt that you're a proud father of a beautiful baby, but deep down you feel like reaching for the panic button. To on-lookers things on the surface might seem okay, but underneath you're paddling like mad to stay afloat and one step ahead of a child with immediate needs. Bottles, baths and the horrid brown stuff that diapers catch only add to the mayhem. Yep, been there, done that and got the T-shirt to prove it. Welcome to the wonderful world of fatherhood.

While the term *father* might be a title of endearment for our children, it should carry some kind of public health warning that reads: *FATHERHOOD: May seriously affect your mental health and sense of physical well-being. Should not be undertaken lightly without first consulting a doctor, minister, bank manager and therapist, as this role will invade your privacy, test your sanity and irreversibly damage your prosperity.*

Although there's much to recommend it, becoming a father is at times incredibly challenging. While the biological side of becoming a parent is in most cases relatively easy and pleasurable, the practical challenge of journeying our children through infancy, adolescence and into adulthood is a highway peppered with potholes. To lovingly and consistently care, cajole, conduct and challenge our children through every stage of life is a commitment for which most of us feel ill-equipped. Yet *fatherhood* is undoubtedly the most significant career choice men will ever make in their lives.

Be it a son or daughter, a genuine father sees them all as priceless pictorial masterpieces set in a frame of precious memories which he will treasure forever. A timely hug, an appreciative look, a thoughtful word, a loving smile, a shared tear, a common laugh, a cherished card, an inspired letter are but a few of the unforgettable moments freeze-framed in the mind of every guy who's a committed dad. And, although the difficult times may be painful reminders of the mistakes we've made, the reality is that "children are God's best gift."[8] This alone should be enough to challenge each of us to at least try to work towards being the best dad we can be, even if we aren't "practically perfect in every way"!

Make-Believe or Reality?

Comic book superheroes were as popular when I was growing up as they've become nowadays, but the one who stood out among the rest back then was Superman. Living as mild-mannered Clark Kent, he would run into the nearest phone booth when necessary, suddenly change into his supersonic hero garb, and save the day. However, when it comes to fatherhood, no matter how commendable the task, there's often a huge gap between make-believe and reality.

In the pursuit of becoming some kind of supersonic parent, we can subconsciously create a caricature of fatherhood that's nothing more than a figment of our own imagination. Some fathers believe that there are guys who instantaneously become dads par-excellence, sort of like Clark Kent changing into Superman, mega-men of whom the world is not worthy.

Fathers who feel that way think these cool, calm, collected captains of industry can answer a phone, finish a report, sip a Starbucks, kick a ball, prepare a bottle, mend a leaky faucet,[9] and attend their kid's ball game—all without breaking into a sweat, staining their immaculate appearance, or "losing it" with the kids, wife or family pet. Like some personification of a comic book superhero, these titans of fatherhood put the rest of us to shame—or so it would appear.

More myth than man, such individuals are the stuff of movie and media hype; they simply don't exist. The idea that every other dad is making it where we're missing it is a fallacy, and the mental creation of a supersonic father is something best left to the comic books.

In our attempts to parent children, we all occasionally get it wrong, make mistakes, and blow a fuse. Yet, if we insist on setting the bar unrealistically high, we'll continually fall short of what we perceive as the goal and be left battling with those thoughts of inadequacy that conclude, "I'm a deadbeat dad who lacks the ability to fulfill the role of a 'perfect father.'" Maybe, just maybe, we have the wrong concept of perfection.

Resolving to do better than our own dads did at fatherhood, most guys set about the task with the best of intentions. Although my own father was, in many areas, a great role model, his approach to fatherhood was a by-product of the Industrial Revolution in which dads were seen as the provider-protector and a "'Wait-till-your-father-gets-home" type of disciplinarian. In this environment, moms were often seen as the senior partner in most aspects of discipline and everyday childcare, while dads were pushed to the periphery of parenting. This, in turn, left my own Baby Boomer style of fathering a tenuous tightrope walk between the distant-dad-provider model of my father's generation and the more hands-on-man-about-the-house style of my son's generation.

Regardless of the method, we all make mistakes. While some are short-term and easily remedied, others may take time to resolve. The reason is that with the arrival of children, most parents find themselves sailing in uncharted waters; with no chance of a dress rehearsal, fatherhood becomes a challenge for which few of us feel totally prepared.

I for one was a novice the first time I became a father in my twenties. I would love to go back to that time with what I know now on being a dad. I would seize every precious opportunity I had to spend time with my children, to embrace those never-to-be-repeated, heart-stopping, earth-shattering, heaven-rending split seconds of time that life is always trying to steal away from us. For in my endeavor to be the best provider-protector my children could possibly know, I didn't realize that the good was robbing me of the great, as I pursued what I believed to be perfection.

Musicians practice for a perfect performance, body builders work for a perfect body, and jewelers dream of a perfect gem, but maybe perfection is not all it's cracked up to be. We talk of a "seamless recital," a "perfect physique," and a "flawless diamond"; but, in terms of perfection, history has dealt humanity a horrid blow causing our judgment to be fundamentally flawed. Siding with the ancient Greek philosophers, many of us have been duped into believing a half-truth.

A Journey of Completing

Like a two-sided coin, perfection does, on the one hand, carry the idea of "something that could not be bettered." Yet, no matter how perfect the performance, possession or person, someone or something is always going to better it—and that to me is the paradox of perfection.

When we accept that only God cannot be bettered, we have to conclude that true perfection is only found in the divine.

With that understanding, thinking of perfection as a journey of *continuous improvement* is encouraging; but to believe in the possibility of arriving at a destination at which someone or something could not be bettered is not only wrong, it is extremely harmful. To bring balance to the argument we need to see perfection from a biblical perspective. When the New Testament refers to someone or something being *perfect*, it is more often than not talking about that person, object or event completing the purpose for which it was intended.

The Bible talks about humans reaching *maturity*, plants coming to *fruition*, and time achieving *fullness*, all of which could equally be spoken of as *becoming perfect*. For instance, an apple tree grows, produces blossoms and looks beautiful, but not until that tree produces fruit has it truly reached the potential for which the Creator intended. Could those apples be bettered by another apple tree? Of course they could, yet we're not looking at perfection in those terms, but rather in terms of the fulfillment of the purpose for which something was initially created. Biblical *perfection* for humans is more a matter of a continuous journey than a final destination. It's when we take the final destination scenario that life suddenly becomes more about *competing* than it does *completing*. Let me explain.

An athlete takes to the track to run the 100 meter Olympic final. Standing in his allotted lane, he begins to ready himself for the race by squatting in his starting blocks. With tunneled vision he fixes his eyes upon the finish line. Months of training all come down to the next few never-to-be-repeated minuscule moments of time. He is ready to complete the course that has been given to him and, having crossed the finished line, receive the gold medal. All that lies between him and the prize is a mere 100 meters of track.

If only that were true! Unfortunately for him, completing is not enough—he has to compete against seven other world-class Olympians. In the realm of track events, being the best you possibly can be and completing the course is not enough, for a runner has to *compete* as well as *complete*. An Olympic runner has to take on all comers and, although he is being the best he can be, it's possible that others will beat him to the prize by a mere bat-of-the-eye measurement of time.

Sadly, when it comes to being a perfect parent, some of us see life in the same way as the Olympic runner. Rather than buying into the truth, we buy the lie that says we're competing against every other seemingly supersonic dad in town to become the one and only "World's Greatest Father." This, in turn, causes us to wrongly compare ourselves with others,[10] when God's purpose is that we run the race He has allotted to us and complete our course in life.

God has not called us to a perfectionism that is competitive. He has called us to draw from His grace and run our race with the strength and ability He has given us.

In this way we can complete the purpose for which we were intended in the best way possible. Just as the apostle Paul, nearing the end of his life, could say, "I have finished *my* course,"[11] unlike the Olympic runner we're not here to compete with others but to complete our allotted course so that, as fathers, we each "run with endurance the race that is set before *us*."[12]

Comparing yourself with others will always leave you feeling a lesser man. By all means admire, appreciate and learn from those who are doing an outstanding job as fathers, but realize that you must run your individual race, stay in the lane God has designated for you, and use those abilities, opportunities and resources He has made available to you to be your best. No matter how good a father you may or may not be, there will always be someone who is better; but being the best *you* possibly could be is all God asks of you.

What Men Really Want

When it comes to becoming dynamic dads, most guys have read the articles, bought the books, and heard the sermons, but the dream still seems as allusive as ever. We've been intimidated as the media parade their latest candidates for Father of the Year, which often leaves us feeling useless, pathetic and as if we're making snail-like progress to better ourselves. Struggling with low self-esteem and a poor self-image, many of us conclude that there is no way we'll ever measure up to this image of the Perfect Father. However, there's a biblical character named David who can empathize with us.

In the prelude to fighting the giant Goliath, King Saul proceeded to place the full weight of his own armor on the young lad David. Loaded down with someone else's preconceived ideas and expectations of how to battle giants, David was left feeling totally overwhelmed.[13] There was no way he could step into Saul's shoes and measure up. He was a 44 Long and David a 38 Short.

Saul was trying to tell David what he should do, but in refusing Saul's kind offer David was saying, "Difference is not wrong, it's just different, and I must place my faith in God *and what works for me.*" David hadn't practiced with Saul's armor; he wasn't perfected at using it. So David determined to be the man God had destined him to be by using what he was familiar with—a slingshot, some stones and his faith.

Fatherhood is not a matter of fulfilling someone else's dreams and expectations, but rather, by God's grace, making the most of who He created us to be. Embracing the strengths and other characteristics our heavenly Father has woven into our lives when we were conceived in our mother's womb[14] is the beginning of becoming perfect in all that God intended for us *individually*. And that is the point—you have to *begin* somewhere.

David began small, working his way up to defeating Goliath and being a young champion by first fighting and killing a lion and a bear while caring for his father's sheep.[15] Becoming a better dad may mean starting small, but there's nothing wrong with small beginnings.[16] Mothers make a physical and psychological bond with their children from the moment of conception, but fathers have to work at it. The more you work at fatherhood, the better you'll get at it, and God will bless your efforts.

Being a good dad, then, isn't a matter of being what you're not; it's knowing that, with God's help, you can make the most of what you are!

Much of the time trying to be a good father is a struggle. We need to be David types who, placing our faith in God, run headlong through our fears and with a few stones of divine truth and a slingshot of proven ability "lay aside every weight, and sin which clings so closely, and...run with endurance the race that is set before us, looking to Jesus, the founder and perfecter of our faith."[17]

Fatherhood is a marathon, not a hundred yard dash—a journey of discovery in which we will undoubtedly trip up and make mistakes. When society seems more skilled at smelling the smoke than extinguishing fires, what men really want is an encouraging word, a friendly face, a listening ear and, when necessary, an offer to help as they attempt one of the most difficult jobs in the world. This book came out of that realization.

My own attempts at fathering have often fallen far short of the characters outlined in the pages to come, but in a day where kids are plugged into every conceivable piece of electronic wizardry known to man and are being bombarded at every turn to believe what the non-Christian culture believes, the one connection they all need is with their father.

There is no such thing as a perfect parent or, for that matter, a perfect child. So whether you are doing brilliantly or badly at fatherhood, don't be intimidated by all you know or don't know about being a dad. As we continue on into the ten characteristics of good fathering, remember that this message is written to be an encouraging word, not a download of weighty expectations, with one sole purpose in mind: to inspire and equip you to be the best you can be and walk in the fullness of all that God has for you as a father.

THE CAVALIER FATHER

Leading a family through the chaos of American culture is like leading a small patrol through enemy-occupied territory.

Steve Farrar[1]

Determining to Be a Dad
Who Leads the Way

picture, as the old cliché goes, is worth a thousand words. That's certainly true of those who report back from the battlefront. As a young man growing up in the sixties, I can still remember the pictures published by the British media that graphically detailed the Vietnam War. Forty years later those images are still a haunting reminder of the horrors of armed conflict. Yet from all the reports and war stories, no picture can truly describe the psychological and physical trauma of guerilla warfare. Movies like *Platoon, Full Metal Jacket* and *Hamburger Hill* tried, but no war correspondent's camera or Hollywood movie can fully encapsulate what it meant to be a soldier fighting the Viet Cong.

It didn't take the American Armed Forces long to realize that the tactics of World War II were no longer a viable option against the North Vietnamese army. Superior firepower and large marching units that could be heard for miles would no longer cut it. This was jungle warfare, and to engage the enemy in his own backyard would mean learning a whole new set of survival techniques to suit the Allied Forces' surroundings. Convinced that smaller, well-armed camouflaged units would be able to move undetected through the undergrowth, the American army began to create small groups of hand-picked, experienced volunteers that could patrol swiftly and silently through the forest.

A new skill they had to learn was to follow the lead of their point man. These were the soldiers who went ahead of their units. Recognized as the most dangerous place in any patrol, the one who walked point took his role extremely seriously for he knew that the lives of those who followed were dependent on his ability to lead.

Risking his own life, the point man carefully searched the way ahead. This was enemy territory and the ability to spot hidden danger and remain undetected was something each soldier would soon learn. It was said of this new breed of fighter that they "moved at a slower pace, nobody smoked, nobody talked above a whisper." Using hand signals as their preferred means of communication, "silence and invisibility were [their] best weapons."

Watching the men walking point has been likened to "watching a puff of smoke maneuver through the dense foliage, disturbing nothing while meticulously observing everything in front of them."[2] As a "fighting family" each man owed his life to the dedication of the one who volunteered to take the lead and walk point on behalf of the rest.

In military terms a point man assumes the foremost exposed

position in any fighting unit. He literally puts himself in harm's way for the sake of others. He sets the pace, senses danger, and makes a safe passage in which others can follow so they can reach their desired destination. In terms of family, the point man illustrates the role and responsibility of all dads, as he takes on the characteristics of the *Cavalier* (or "go-before") *Father*.

Leading the Way

The apostle Paul's statement in the New Testament that nature itself teaches us[3] is so true, as in the case of Canadian geese. These magnificent creatures offer men some valuable life lessons on being *Cavalier Fathers* and walking point for our families. The geese fly in V formation for a reason. Scientists have discovered that the flapping action of each bird creates uplift for those following. As a strong adult bird takes the position of point, others honk sounds of encouragement while following in the wake of his lead. By staying in formation, a flock can increase their flying range by at least seventy percent. If, for some reason, a bird happens to fall out of formation, the drag and resistance felt from flying solo and the loss of the lift provided by others quickly brings the stray bird back into line.

The formation flying of geese is fascinating. Yet it's the importance of taking the lead, offering encouraging words, and creating uplift (in our case an uplifting environment) that should speak volumes to those of us who, by desire or default, find ourselves being called Dad. More than ever before, families need men who will position themselves at the forefront and lead in a way that gives vision, values and vitality to all who follow.

Every child needs a father, a male role model they can look up to, a special someone who will lead by example while offering words of encouragement along the way (just as migrating geese do by honking). In this kind of loving environment, a child experiences the necessary lift to pursue their own destiny in life. And if for some reason a child decides to prematurely go it alone, the drag and resistance they feel flying solo should be enough to encourage them to find their way back into the formation of a loving family, led by a loving father.

Although the concept of a cavalier, go-before, walking point father may be thought by some to be a relatively modern means of leadership, it's actually traceable as far back as Bible times. The ancient Jewish nation, known as the children of Israel, undertook a forty year long march through enemy territory while being led by the one true God, their (and our) heavenly Father, who Himself implemented the strategy of the go-before dad. By means of a pillar of cloud by day and a pillar of fire by night, our Father God walked point for His people, while they in turn had to learn to place their trust in His ability to lead.

In a classic book on the wilderness life, *Made According to Pattern,* C. W. Slemming portrays the children of Israel as some ancient nomadic Bedouin tribe moving through the desert, with their chieftain seen "leading the way on his camel or Arab steed and carrying in his hand his spear…. When the chieftain wanted to settle his camp for a while he would just plant his spear into the ground…. His servants would immediately erect their master's tent behind the spear and pitch their tents around [their leader's tent].... The sheik then dwelt in the midst of his people. When he desired to move on, he removed the spear and rode forth."[4] In the same way, God spearheaded His children through uncharted territory and, in so doing, created the concept of a "God who goes before"[5] – the heavenly Father present 24/7 to provide and protect while offering safe passage for those who followed His fatherly lead.

In these biblical snapshots, we begin to understand this vital aspect of fatherhood I call the *Cavalier Father*. The term *cavalier* is used in the positive sense of being a *courageous, chivalrous, valiant solider who leads the charge* and not in the negative sense of being offhanded, supercilious and proud. When a father walks point and by example makes a way in which his children safely follow, he is in the true sense of the word being *cavalier* – one who leads the charge in all things moral, spiritual, social and financial for his family.

We who are dads are called to walk point for each of our children – to take the lead and secure a safe passage through the jungle called life – no matter the opposition we might face.

Walking the Point

In true cavalier style, a father named Augusto Odone led the charge for a cure for his son in the face of great opposition. Augusto had received a grim diagnosis from the medical establishment concerning his boy but was unwilling to accept the doctor's prognosis that his child had an incurable disease and had less than two years to live. Now in his twenties, Augusto's son is a living witness to the power of having a father who was willing to walk point.

With no scientific training whatsoever, this father (and his wife) never gave up hope of a possible cure. Undeterred by the doctor's unwillingness to help, he "spent night after night in the library scouring every single paper about his son's illness. He discovered that the brain damage seemed to be linked to a buildup of dangerous fatty acids in the blood."[6] As a nonmedical person, he went as far as inviting the world experts on this particular disease to attend a conference to discuss his research so that in less than a year a viable treatment was found.

Where the entire medical profession had failed, a husband and wife team succeeded as they willingly put themselves in the line of fire for their son. Beautifully portrayed in the Hollywood movie, *Lorenzo's Oil*, this is the story of a *Cavalier Father* who inspires others to make a way for their children to reach a desired destination.

Braving the societal elements to lead from the front is a strong skill of this father character. By leading he protects his family from the sniper fire and possible ambush of a culture whose divisive tactics are aimed at dividing and destroying the family as we know it. Never asking others to do what he himself is not willing to do, as point man he searches for those moral, spiritual, social and financial booby traps set by the enemy. Willing to do whatever it takes to regain lost territory, the *Cavalier Father* is a much needed breed of man. Yet, although protective of his children and constantly guiding and guarding their way through life, he is never knowingly so overly protective that he wraps his precious treasures in the cotton wool of spiritual isolation or social ignorance.

Cocooning

Arthur Blessitt has literally walked the face of the earth — 38,000 miles over a period of 38 years — sharing the message of Jesus to every nation and major island group throughout the world. Carrying a large wooden cross, he's hiked across deserts, hacked his way through jungles, walked through inner city ghettos, entered war-zones and gained access to nations closed to tourists, believing that "people in all cultures respond to the cross."[7]

There's something else perhaps even more amazing about Arthur. He's always encouraged his seven children to experience for themselves the stark realities of this world and the way in which God can provide and protect those on a heavenly mission to some of the most inhospitable countries on earth. Like the time Arthur took his eleven-year-old son, Joshua, into the war-torn Middle East.

When, in the summer of 1982, war broke out between Israel and the Palestinian Liberation Organization, Arthur knew he had to revisit Yasser Arafat, head of the PLO. Believing God had asked him to accompany his father, Joshua asked to go with him. Using the whole experience as a teaching moment, father and son traveled into one of the most dangerous places on the planet. The media even captured a picture of the PLO leader standing between this father and son team who each carried their own cross, while Arthur prayed for Yasser Arafat.

Not every *Cavalier Father* will want to walk through a minefield, cross check-points or enter a battlefield with their children as Arthur did, but these dads have a desire to do whatever it takes to insulate rather than isolate their kids from the realities of life. The antithesis of the *Cavalier Father* is the *Cocooning Father*, the man who overly protects his children from all adverse outside influences.

Faith Popcorn, an author and marketing consulting firm CEO, coined the word *cocooning* and described it as, "the impulse to go *inside* when it just gets too tough and scary *outside*."[8] *Cocooning* as a dad is when we pull up the drawbridge to our castles and keep our children totally removed from this nasty, scary, unpredictable world.

Maintaining balance is essential to good parenting, but the *Cocooning Father* not only makes the mistake of paying too much attention to his children; he becomes too involved in their lives, choosing to live his own life through their behavior and achievements. This intense style of parenting handicaps his kids' ability to develop into who God destined them to become, and usually causes them to end up overly dependent on Dad and Mom.

The home is supposed to be a secure environment in which parents exercise godly authority to raise their children to adulthood, yet the time comes when they have to release those adult children, to make their own mark in the world. Nature teaches us this through the eagle. As majestic and magnificent as an eagle might appear to be, there comes a point that even a young eagle needs a push to leave the nest. Likening God to a parent eagle, the Old Testament character Moses speaks of how eagles exercise tough love by breaking up the eaglets' comfort zones. All of this for one purpose—to force them to stretch their wings, exercise their inherent ability, and soar to new heights.[9]

A *Cocooning Father* doesn't want anything to warp the young minds of his children, so his protectionist style tends to shelter and separate them from a post-Christian culture to the extent that they are incapable of functioning well on their own in society. These children soon become "institutionalized" by a Christian Club mentality that does little to prepare them for life in the real world. The children of *cocooners* can easily become totally irrelevant to a lost and dying world seeking answers. Just as the religious people ignored the battered and bruised man in the New Testament story of the Good Samaritan,[10] these kids tend to live sterile lives that avoid anything or anyone who might contaminate them.

Because of the world's reputation, they choose to not even take the Jericho Road. Instead, they travel through life on some "holier than thou" moral highway. More *isolated* than *insulated* from this world, the children of *Cocooning Fathers* live life in a religious bubble. Some people make things happen and others watch things happen, but these kids in all probability say at the end of their lives, "What happened?"

David Hempleman-Adams is an explorer extraordinaire.

He has climbed the highest peaks on all seven continents, successfully walked 300 miles to the Geomagnetic North Pole, solo and unsupported, hauling his Kevlar sled and walking the last 100 miles with a broken ankle. This is a man who takes risks. In the summer of 1999, he spoke to the Royal Geographic Society, voicing his concern that many of us have become overprotective of our children and prevent them from ever being risk-takers.

Concerned that expedition leaders, teachers and parents were abandoning field trips and expeditions because of their fears of possible accidents and lawsuits, the Society had called a meeting of interested parties. Hempleman-Adams spoke there, saying, "We are becoming a nation of softies...[who are] surrounding our children in cotton wool...they will not be able to cope with the risk when they encounter it as adults."[11]

I might not want my children to attempt an unsupported solo walk across the North Pole or ski down Everest, but I do want them to have a willingness to step out of the boat of social conformity and take a calculated risk—not to be a rebel without a cause but to find a cause, worth dying for and give their life for it. Sadly, *Cocooning Fathers* have, in their overly protective mind-set, created a ghetto mentality that keeps their children ignorant as to how they can be world changers. In the case of "cocooning" fathers, this isolationism is born out of a protection that is both unbiblical and unhealthy. Christianity is God's alternative culture. Christians are not here to be shaped by the world; *we*, by God's grace, are supposed to shake the world and shape it.

Overprotecting our kids may be safe, but it sure isn't sound.

To not allow "the world to squeeze you into its mould"[12] is one thing, but when we are petrified of our children becoming *infected* by this world, we are at the same time stopping them from being *affected* by it. They should be affected by the fact that 21 children under the age of five die each minute somewhere in the world mainly from preventable diseases and poverty; that half the world's population live on less than $2 a day; that 40 billion people are living with HIV/AIDS;[13] and that thousands of people die daily without hearing the Christian message of hope through Jesus Christ—which is, perhaps, the most important mandate a Christian Father can instill in his children.

Cocooning Fathers ultimately stifle and suppress their children; *Cavalier Fathers* lead the charge in giving their kids a cause to live and die for because they have grown to realize that the greatest danger in life is to miss the adventure.

Taking the Adventure

Impressed by his adventurous spirit, I decided to attend the book signing of a 53-year-old Yorkshire man who had recently climbed Mount Everest. Brian Blessed is a well-known English actor who has appeared in numerous British television series and feature films, notably as Voltan the warrior chief in *Flash Gordon*. Brian's passion to climb was secondary to his life-long ambition to follow in the steps of his hero, George Mallory. Blessed's book, *The Turquoise Mountain*, was published to coincide with the release of his film *Galahad of Everest*.

Having dutifully lined up with other customers, I suddenly

found myself face to face with the man himself. With a friendly smile and genuine word of greeting, he inquired as to my own interests. When I said that I was working on my first book on the subject of attitudes, he began telling me a pertinent story about George Mallory and his final ascent of Everest in 1924.

As Mallory was about to leave the safe environment of his home for the Himalayas, newspaper reporters questioned him as to the wisdom of his decision to climb Everest, knowing that he would be leaving his wife and children. These journalists asked if he didn't feel that the adventure was too dangerous, to which Mallory replied, "Yes it is dangerous going to Mount Everest. But the greatest danger in life is not taking the adventure."[14]

Fathers ought to do whatever we can to give our children a sense of adventure, to break out of the cotton wool syndrome that has boxed up the passion for being and the creative potential in so many kids. For a lot of young people, the right of passage into adulthood will be marred, as well-meaning but overprotective parents do not allow their children to *take the adventure.* A few years ago well-known author Richard Paul Evans gave his daughter the adventure of a lifetime:

"I took my oldest daughter, Jenna, on a daddy-daughter date to the Amazon jungles of Peru on a humanitarian mission. I wanted her to not only realize how much we have to be grateful for, but to learn to serve others who are less fortunate. Our journey turned into an extraordinary adventure. We hiked deep into the jungle with machetes, and at one point we ran out of food. The only meat we had was piranha.... We set up a clinic in the small jungle town of Puerto Maldonada, and the Quechuan natives came from miles around."

About two weeks later, when the trip was over, Richard asked Jenna what she had learned from the experience. It actually took her twelve hours to ponder that question before she answered, but when she finally did, she was crying. "'Dad,' she said, 'we have so much and they have so little.' She looked down for a moment, then added, 'I know what I've learned. We love those whom we serve.'"[15]

A *Cavalier Father* may not be a type T personality who loves to jump out of airplanes at 13,000 feet to experience the thrill of free falling, or who hangs off a sheer cliff-face in order to get a rush and release endorphins, or who machetes his way through the deep jungle and eats piranha; but he can still do everything possible to nurture a spirit of adventure in his children.

Of course, there will be times when it's necessary for the *Cavalier Father* to draw a line in the sand to stop his kids in their tracks and warn them of the consequences of certain choices they are about to make that are too dangerous. Although all children test the parameters, they find comfort in fathers who will love them enough to say no. Every child needs a dad who is strong enough in his decision-making process that he avoids the possibility of sending mixed messages to those who follow. Refusing to shrink, shirk or shy away from his responsibility, the *Cavalier Father* will, if necessary, take a stand for the absolutes of biblical truth, knowing that parenthood is not a popularity competition, but rather a walking point to show others the way forward.

We live in enemy territory. The world is a cover-up job that front's destructive forces out to cultivate and sow disruptive seeds into the fertile minds of our children.[16] Camouflaged by the foliage of liberal thinking and the undergrowth of years of humanistic mindsets, what seems innocent and inconspicuous often hides a more sinister agenda. Much of what passes as acceptable is often a covert operation to influence our children with an ideology that is blatantly opposed to a Judeo-Christian belief system.

Children don't need parents whose disclaimer in life is, "Do as I say, not as I do." They need adult role models, mentors who will take them by the hand and lead them in the ways of God.

When a father sits down to preview something his child might watch, he is walking point. When a dad pre-reads questionable material being handed out by educational institutions, he is taking the lead so as to avoid a possible ambush from subversive thinkers who are covertly seeking to prey on young minds. When a father steps in to lovingly challenge a poor choice being made by an older child, he is drawing a line in the sand and acting as only a loving father should.

Fathers can't afford to be laid back in their approach to parenting. The *Cavalier Father* does his best to build character in his kids by being passionate in his role and responsibility as a way-maker and family leader. He may feel like a lone voice crying in the wilderness, but society *and his family* desperately need to see a positive change in the way the world characterizes fatherhood. That's going to take consistency and commitment from guys of all cultural backgrounds—men who are setting the pace by resolutely maintaining the kind of work/home life balance that walks point for their families and takes the lead in breaking the cycle of fathers who aren't.

 Personal Reflections

• Can you think of an example where either you or another father has acted as a point man for his children?

• Are you the kind of father who takes the lead or someone who tends to hang back? If you hang back, what's your strategy for change?

• Do you tend to *cocoon* or *isolate* your children in a way that will possibly handicap their development? Why, or why not?

• On a scale of 1—10, how observant are you to possible moral booby traps, social landmines and vocal sniper fire aimed at taking your kids out of their pursuit of the Christian faith?

 Group Discussion

• What aspects of the *Cavalier Father* have challenged you the most, and why?

• How do you intend to improve in areas of weakness and maintain areas of strength?

THE COACH FATHER

Good coaches and good fathers have similar goals. Both involve teaching and trying to get the best out of individuals, getting them to play up to their potential.

Tony Dungy, Head Coach, Indianapolis Colts[1]

Determining to Be a Dad
Who Develops Potential

Wimbledon reigns supreme in the world of lawn tennis. The epitome of everything English, the annual Wimbledon Lawn Tennis Championship has, over the years, held players and spectators spellbound as they've observed the magic of the world's greatest pros. Australian tennis player Rod Laver held his ranking as World No. 1 for seven consecutive years and is the only tennis player to have twice won all four Grand Slam singles titles in the same year. Rated by some as the greatest male player of all time, Laver dominated world lawn tennis for more than a decade — along with his archrival Ken Rosewall.

At 5 feet, 7 inches tall and weighing in at 145 pounds, Ken Rosewall did not have your average physique for a world number one tennis player but, like Rod Laver, he owed much of his success to the expertise of his coach, Henry Christian Hopman. Known to his friends simply as "Harry," he was a man who had the uncanny skill of seeing and securing the very best in his players.

In an effort to awaken the latent potential he had observed in young Rod, Harry nicknamed him "Rocket." A slow, short, scrawny-looking kid, Laver was anything but a rocket, yet Harry perceived potential and encapsulated it in the boy's new name. Some have suggested that Laver's nickname was given to counterbalance his tendency to be lazy and inconsistent in using his inherent speed and agility. Whatever the truth, Harry's vision for Rod "Rocket" Laver helped turn this skinny kid into a superstar who dominated the world of men's tennis in the early 1960s.

The epitome of coaching expertise, Harry would challenge his players to be the best they possibly could be. Maybe to offset his lack of physical strength, some reckon that it was Harry who gave Ken Rosewall the nickname of "Muscles." Another of Harry's world-beating protégés, Rosewall also would become one of the top male tennis players of all time.

Whether the names *Rocket* or *Muscles* were used cynically or constructively, I like to believe that both were given by a fatherly coach recognizing latent talent in his "kids." Harry was a man who sought, by whatever positive and legitimate means possible, to encourage them to become their very best and reach their full potential, which personifies the next character trait of a dad — the *Coach Father*.

If you are a father you may not be aware that, according to medical science, out of 500 million sperm who tried to get through to create a child, only one succeeded. That's what you might call a *winner*! Nine months later the miracle of birth presents us with a heavenly gift of pure, unadulterated potential we call a baby. Ready or not, this bundle of joy bursts into our world with desires and demands that make the choice of fathering a child a living reality. And remember, being a father is the job of a lifetime — literally.

Shouldering the responsibility for our share in the development of these living, screaming, smiling parcels of possibility is something no man must ever take lightly. Each precious life innocently awaits the impact of those positive and negative influences he or she is yet to encounter. At first, that would-be masterpiece is cradled in the easel of our care — an empty canvas yet to be colored by the pallet of life's experiences, a blank page that will find perspective and definition through the brush strokes of a family and the artistry of a father.

A 'Mona Lisa,' a Sistine Chapel, a *magnum opus* (Latin for "great work")[2] is in the making of each young pliable life yet to be shaped by people, objects, events and, most of all, by his or her father. As a jeweler sees the hidden potential within an uncut gemstone or a sculptor visualizes the magnificent human form in a piece of quarried marble, a father can discover the diverse beauty and endless possibility in every one of his children and help to mold them into priceless treasures.

Getting into Partnership

King David was the father of many children, so it's understandable how he could write lyrics in the Psalms of amazing truths about kids, as in "Children are God's best gift,"[3] and each one is "fearfully and wonderfully made."[4] David prefaced that profound verse with words of praise: "You shaped me first inside, then out; you formed me in my mother's womb. I thank you, High God — you're breathtaking!"[5] I believe what took David's breath away was this incredible image of God forming, weaving, knitting and embroidering us in our mother's womb. David pictured God as the divine weaver intricately piecing us together like one who embroiders a piece of needlework.

Another Old Testament father named Job put it like this, "You clothed me with skin and flesh, and knit me together with bones and sinews."[6] God shaped us inside and out, giving us individual features by which we are recognized as the unique irreplaceable *us*. This has been aptly described as "God's imprint on each of us," those unique features that "have seemingly infinite possibilities when rearranged in different shapes and sizes," and are "wonderfully made."[7]

What if the divine weaver embroidered more than those physical features into our human form? What if, knowing our purpose in life, He added an extra dash of color in certain areas, so as to equip us for the particular journey He alone has called us to walk? We describe someone as being a "colorful character," so what if God's "multicolored grace"[8] or multifaceted giftedness is something He divinely weaves into our lives when we are being "embroidered" in our mother's womb?

What of quiet, unassuming individuals? Are they any less a work of the divine weaver than more talented and outgoing kids? Can we say of children whose lives are colored with a more pastel shade of personality, their physical form not like others, their giftedness more muted, that God failed to brush stroke into them what is so evident in others? No, for there is beauty in every piece of fabric, no matter how frail or fraught with challenges. But, typical of our human perspective on life, we often tend to observe the gift wrapping instead of taking the time to discover the touch of the divine weaver in all human beings.

As *Coach Fathers* we're called to discover and develop those multifaceted and colorful elements embroidered into each of our children so as to encourage them to use every color divinely woven into their God-given palette. By cultivating our children's strengths, corralling their weaknesses, acknowledging their abilities, and applauding their every effort, *Coach Fathers* lead in a way that enables kids to become all that God created them to be.

Think of the incredible privilege we have as dads — to partner with our maker in forming this multifaceted life that could refract the brilliance of God in all that our children say and do throughout their lives! Although the developmental process takes an inordinate amount of time, effort and expense, it all begins when a father recognizes the endless possibilities hidden in each of his children and works at "coaching" them to bring out the best in those areas.

Movers and Influencers

There's no doubt about it, *coaching* (as a discipline to bring the best out of a person) is an "in" word, but not a new one. History tells us that *coaching,* or what might be better termed *mentoring,* used to happen primarily in the home. Children were coached by their parents or extended family. It was Mom and Dad who gave their kids that sense of maleness and femaleness and taught them the basic life skills--a good work ethic, character, duty and responsibility. In fact, it's a father that history honors with the introduction of this concept of *mentoring.*

Homer's *Odyssey* describes how King Odysseus entrusted the training of his son Telemachus to a man called Mentor, while he himself went off to war. This ancient Greek text gives us valuable insight into the character of a *Coaching Father*, for in Mentor we see someone entrusted with the responsibility of guarding and guiding a young life through his formative years, to bring the best out of him.

We live in a time when parents spend an average of eight to eleven minutes a day conversing with their children. It's no wonder there's an explosion of previously unknown coaching job descriptions: *life coach, career coach, business coach, personal coach, health coach* and *dating coach,* to name a few. Yet, in spite of this being the twenty-first century, the nature of true parental coaching still must be done in the home.

Parents need to remain the prime movers and chief influencers in every developmental aspect of their children's lives. When a dad abdicates his responsibility as number one trainer, his actions not only create a learning vacuum that could, in time, implode under the pressure to conform, but his absence can open the door for undesirables to step in and influence his child's life.

The apostle Paul wrote on fatherhood in the New Testament book of Ephesians, saying: "Fathers, do not provoke your children to anger, but bring them up in the *discipline* and instruction of the Lord."[9] The Greek word for "discipline" here is *paideia* and could equally be understood as meaning "education."[10] Yet Paul's not talking about our kids having a formal education provided by the state, a local Sunday school, or a morning family devotion. Those things are good, but he's referring to fathers being the primary movers in teaching their children the ways of God in all things physical, mental, social and spiritual.

Paul is urging every dad to become personally involved in the training of his children—to coach them in the ways of the kingdom so that eventually they will become fully-fledged members of God's counter-culture, the church, and thereby be ready to influence a post-Christian culture with their godly lifestyle. We're talking educating for excellence, teaching our children the ways of God in all that we say and do with them. Be it in the classroom or on the golf course, fathers are not called to abdicate our responsibility to others. *We're called to take every opportunity to coach our children in such a way that enables them to excel for the kingdom of God.*

Acting as a mentor or *Coach Father,* Paul urged his spiritual son, Timothy, to *"train* yourself for godliness."[11] The word he uses for "train" is the word from which we get our English word "gymnasium."[12] He saw the potential in Timothy and encouraged the young man to exercise those spiritual disciplines that would develop him, to workout in such a way as to grow mentally, physically, spiritually and socially fit,[13] and become a person who is "in shape" to serve the purpose of God in and for his generation. Paul's encouragement and guidance of Timothy illustrates the job God gave to fathers: to be *chiselers* — but in a good way!

Effective Cutting Edge

In a period of history known as B.P. ("Before Power-tools"), woodworkers used instruments that are today more likely to find their way into the Collectables section of eBay than on the shelves of your local hardware store. I actually began my working career using tools that are now conversation pieces, items of historical interest that my grandchildren would probably laugh at. Back then, no self-respecting joiner would find himself without a good set of wood chisels. *Firmer, beveled, swan-necked, mortise* and *pairing* are all familiar chisel names associated with a time when a carpenter's skill involved his ability to use a variety of boxwood-handled, Sheffield steel carpenter's chisels.

Those apprenticing into the world of carpentry soon discovered that the skill required in effectively using any cutting tool was dependent on the time and effort given to sharpening and re-sharpening various pieces of steel. A blunt instrument required more brute force and would often break rather than cut through the fibers of a piece of cross-grained, stubborn and resilient hardwood. So, frequent visits to a well-oiled sharpening stone were necessary to maintain an effective cutting edge. Coaching children is no different. No matter how mixed up, stubborn or resistant to change a child might appear to be, the *Coach Father* must maintain an effective cutting edge in all his coaching activities. I call this *Chisel Coaching*.

The acronym *C-H-I-S-E-L* speaks of six key elements involved in effective coaching: *Challenging, Hearing, Inspiring, Showing, Encouraging* and *Leading* with love those for whom we have been made responsible. We're going to talk about each one because they're all crucial to the proper development of our kids. Yet for them to work, the *Coach Father* first must be functioning effectively himself — maintaining an effective cutting edge to his own life.

Who Do You Call?

No one can deny the importance of time at the sharpening stone. The biblical proverb refers to it as, "Iron sharpens iron, and one man sharpens another."[14] Without accountability we will always tend to lose our cutting edge. Lack of an accountability partner will cause us to become blunt and in danger of using brute force to try and get the job done.

Realizing the danger of bruising and breaking the tender fibers of a child's life, fathers need to take time out with mature mentors whose spiritual interaction will help hone those ineffective aspects of their own life. In this way fathers are the first to be coached so they are *challenged, heard, inspired, shown how, encouraged* and *led lovingly* in the ways of God. As *Coach Fathers*, we'll never develop our children beyond our own ability, so to grow our kids we must grow ourselves by implementing the mentoring model in our own lives.

If you are thinking that you don't need help to raise your own kids, let me ask you a few questions:

■ When overwhelmed by some difficult stage in your child's development that leaves you feeling absolutely useless as a father, who do you call?

■ When your back is against the wall and you lack the right answer or course of action, who do you call?

■ When you've blown it big time with your teenager, who do you call?

■ When drowning in a sea of doubt and unbelief concerning your ability to function as a dad, who do you call?

■ With a tendency to run, rather than face the challenge, who do you call to find the strength to go on?

I don't know about you, but while the theory seems plausible, it's putting it into practice that gets me every time! It feels as if at each turn in the road to effective parenting my theories keep getting mugged by a gang of facts. So when life as a father has seemed totally overwhelming and the way before me blocked by a landslide of circumstances, I have often reached out to others for a helping hand. Only a phone call away, my veteran father-friends have, over the years, empowered me as a parent to face the trauma of "night terrors," "terrible twos" and "teenage tantrums." With a proven track record, these seasoned dads have sharpened my perspective and inspired me to once again pick up those dreams, goals and aspirations I had fostered for each of my children.

Coach Fathers need coaches, people who co-partner with us and are available to renew an edge blunted by a particular situation — mature individuals who can teach us a life lesson in the midst of a trying moment. Yet that's sometimes harder for men than women to initiate, mainly due to our emotional differences.

Operating under this principle my wife, Tina, often recalls memorable moments when one of her friends encouraged her through various difficult parental experiences. Whenever one or all of our four children had driven Tina to a point of desperation and she was left battling a poor self-image and low self-esteem as a mother, she would call her friend and simply say, "Tell me I'm a wonderful mother," and get the response, "You're a wonderful mother," and then her friend would ask, "Now, tell me what you've done." Tina would then relate either the horrors or hoorays of the last few hours, because her friend was someone with whom she could celebrate the wins and commiserate the losses. For special seasons in her life, that coach, mentor, friend was only a phone call away.

Just as a CEO, manager, minister, sports personality or troubled teenager often draws on the expertise of a life-coach to take them to the next level, so every child needs a *Coach Father* to create a nurturing environment in which to cultivate the winning edge necessary to fulfill their potential. Since a *Coach Father* is called to focus on a child's potential while urging them to pursue a perceived goal, no father — married or divorced, stepfather, grandfather, godfather, father-to-be, travelling or stay-at-home father — can afford to overlook the call to coach.

I'm not advocating the time, expertise and expense some dads feel justified in spending in an effort to produce the next sports superstar. I'm referring to the simple task of recognizing our kids' potential and doing whatever it takes to *challenge, hear, inspire, encourage* and *lovingly lead* them in ways that cause them to be the best they can be with the resources life has given them. In this way, the *Coach Father* facilitates rather than forces growth, inspires rather than insists, builds up rather than belittles. Perceiving apparent strengths and weaknesses, he waters the seeds of greatness while constantly cultivating the soil of a fertile mind, so as to remove the weeds of negative influence planted by people, objects and events.

At this point you may be wondering how you could ever be a *Coach Father*. I believe it takes coming back to the relational links of home, family and community life that were enjoyed by our grandparents.

Surrogates and Software

Much of our modern educational system can be traced back to a Judaic model that placed primary responsibility of teaching on parents and saw learning as a joint effort between home and state, but it was ultimately the father's responsibility to see that his children were taught the truth.[15] Yet, although the ancient biblical text has the home as the hallowed place for learning, there is a growing tendency to hand over our God-given responsibility to educate our children to surrogate teachers who too often end up totally substituting for it.

The Chinese language is said to have two characters that represent the word *learning*. The first has the meaning "to study" and is made up of symbolism that means "to accumulate knowledge"; it is illustrated by lettering that represents a child in a doorway. The second set of Chinese characters means "to practice constantly" and is illustrated by symbols showing birds developing the ability to leave the nest. True education is epitomized in both of these, for learning is, first and foremost, the responsibility of parents in the home. This learning is not merely the accumulation of knowledge, but serves to enable children to become mature enough to "fly the nest" and take their place in society, so they can reproduce in others what they've learned from their parents.

The loss of this kind of traditional home and family life has created a generation more likely than any generation before them to find relationships by means of some form of electronic gadgetry, popular music and poor media. While the Google age has much to offer our kids that's good, it should never be seen as a viable alternative to the developmental role of a loyal and loving parent. No matter how we cut it, the home is God's primary place of learning and parents are the principle teachers. Sadly, these practices are no longer part of many homes; instead, "Children are put on auto-pilot each and every day with game systems, television and the Internet as their babysitter."[16]

Fathers (and mothers) who allow surrogates and software to become the primary players in their children's education will live to regret it. The fact is God has called us dads to foster a learning environment in which "[you] talk about [truths] wherever you are, sitting at home or walking in the street; talk about them from the time you get up in the morning to when you fall into bed at night."[17] Rather than giving lip-service to biblical truths, God is charging fathers to make learning a lifestyle. Yet in our busyness to better ourselves, the home has become, in many quarters, the last place children learn biblical principles.

When talking about raising kids, some godly parents love to reach for their "get out clause"' by quoting the verse, "Train up a child in the way he should go; even when he is old he will not depart from it."[18] They forget that the Proverbs are more principle than promise, and they add their own postscript to this scripture that says, "If we '*point* [our] kids in the right direction,'[19] God has guaranteed that they will never depart from the Christian faith. Isn't that right, God?" Not necessarily.

Most Christians either know of or have children who have departed from the faith, kids who no longer follow a godly way of life. When this happens, these parents are often left feeling condemned, believing that in some way it must be their fault; that they somehow failed to follow the required code of practice. True, some kids have been turned off from the Christian life because of their parents' inconsistency; but children make a personal choice to follow or not follow the faith of their parents through no fault of their parents (more on that in the chapter on the *Cinderella Father*).

Probably a majority of children from sound Christian homes decide in due course to follow Christ for themselves, or at least live by broadly Christian standards — but there are exceptions at both ends of the spectrum. Ultimately, salvation is not by osmosis; it is a work of grace by which God alone brings someone to a place of deciding to make Him their CEO, boss or manager, and seeking daily to live the life associated with being a Christ follower.

As parents we should build the right values and practices into our children from an early age, for it is more than likely that they will adhere to those things even when they reach adulthood. Still, we can't armlock God, hoping He will submit to our demands according to our timetable, for His "thoughts are not [our] thoughts, neither are [our] ways [His] ways."[20]

One interpretation of the "train up a child" verse gives a whole new perspective on how we might coach our kids. Some translate it as "train up a child in *his way*,"[21] thereby advocating that parents should find out early on in life what a child's natural talents and temperament are, and develop them accordingly. In this case fathers would need to be more creative in their approach to coaching those unique gifts and abilities they have taken time to observe in their kids. Saying good-bye to the one-size-fits-all approach, a *Coach Father* would need to tailor-make his coaching method to suit his child's particular way of seeing things.

However you interpret this verse, I feel that by adopting a more creative approach to *challenging, hearing, inspiring, showing, encouraging* and *lovingly leading* our children, we can avoid that square-peg-in-a-round-hole syndrome that so many seem to struggle with nowadays.

It's All in the Swing

In order to expand his thinking, American author Leonard Sweet practices what he calls "random reading." Besides bookstores, he also follows the same procedure when attending the cinema or restaurant by asking the server or ticket seller to recommend a good meal or good movie. It's this theory of random selection that has given him some of the incredible eureka moments in his life.

During a recent episode of random selection, he found himself reading an article on both the physics and science of the golf swing. Rather than some boring, unprofitable exercise, the article actually enlightened him regarding a new theory. Be it a child's garden swing or Tiger Woods' golf swing, the article suggested that rather than placing emphasis on the middle of the arc in any swing (or the moment a golfer strikes the ball), we should see the importance and implications of each end of the swing. In simple layman's terms, the physicist noted that the *backward motion* of any swing has a drastic effect on the *forward momentum* of the said swing. In other words, what is behind us always affects what is before us.

We all are products of our past, and history has a bearing on our present and our future. Golfers can ill afford to relegate their backward swing to the realm of insignificant; neither can they place little importance on the follow-through. Both drastically affect the strike of the ball (a theory I prove every time I attempt to hit a golf ball and produce either a hook or slice!). Relating that to fathers, some dads struggle to connect with their children because of what is behind them.

My father was a businessman who gave way too much time and effort to building a successful business, but he still was a positive role model who left me a legacy that far outweighs material wealth. Yet his generation saw things totally different from mine and those of his grandchildren. Dad and I agreed on the absolutes of biblical truth, but in other things we had preferences that were opposite, as in music—he preferred classical and easy listening; I liked rock and roll. We all can *learn* from our past, but we can't afford to overly *lean* on it. My father wore "glasses" that philosophically suited his day, but to wear his glasses now would handicap me in accomplishing what I'm called to do in my day.

With the passage of time, fathers have to change their perspective on things without losing sight of the absolutes of the Judeo-Christian faith. In each new generation, dads need a fresh perspective so they can lead their children with reality and relevance in the ways of God and of life.

Having suffered from the affects of a deadbeat dad or an absentee father, some guys' past can blur their vision of the future. Growing up without a father or with a deadbeat dad has left some men struggling to know how to connect with their children. Other dads' lack of follow-through with promises or set principles hooks or slices their kids off the fairway into the rough on a regular basis.

Be it the inability to put the past in perspective or a poor follow-through on a decision or course of action, we cannot allow these things to affect our role and responsibility as coach fathers. We need to put our past in perspective and adjust our back swing in the same way we need to remedy our lack of follow-through. We've seen one line of attack in doing that: by allowing our accountability partners to observe our attempts at fathering. This is important because poor fathers leave a poor legacy (*legacy* will be covered more in-depth later on) or template; they will produce poor fathers if someone doesn't stop the cycle and correct the mistakes made by previous generations (which we may be inadvertently copying).

In preparation for writing this book, I asked a select group of fathers if they would complete an anonymous fathers' survey. To ascertain what their fathers had left them as a legacy, the question was asked, "What did your dad teach you?" Some of the answers were surprising, others were more sobering.

My dad taught me…

■ Nothing, but by teaching me nothing he taught me something—to be a father, period.

■ Generosity in giving both money and encouragement and the ability to cover other's faults with silence.

■ Strength of character, faithfulness, firm belief in a Christian faith.

■ Responsibility and how to work hard.

■ To live for the moment but to give all of yourself because your today affects your tomorrow.

■ A dying devotion to my mother.

■ To respect others and look for the best in them.

Of all the *father surveys* returned, 99 percent of the answers to this question were to do with *attitude* rather than *aptitude*. Some learned how to play an instrument, catch a ball, repair a car, but the overwhelming majority spoke of how their dads taught them an attitude. I guess the question we as fathers need to ask ourselves is, "What am I teaching my children by the things I say and do?"

Whether we like it or not, we all teach our children something. They learn from our moods, motives, manners and mistakes. Overtly or covertly, we are constantly schooling our kids in the lessons of life. As coach fathers we can strive to make it our goal to give them a living legacy that will equip and facilitate their journey or race, and *insulate* them from the moral, ethical, social, financial and spiritual challenges they will invariably face.

 ## Personal Reflections

• List your children's names and write besides their names what particular talent, temperament and learning style you have observed in them.

• Do you have an accountability partner who asks you the hard questions and is available if you call? If not, what can you do to get one?

• What element of your 'back swing' or 'follow-through' in fathering, if any, are you struggling with and how do you intend to address it?

 ## Group Discussion

Of the six elements of "Chisel Coaching"—*challenging, hearing, inspiring, showing, encouraging* and *leading* your children with love—which one are you finding the most difficult? How do you hope the following chapters will help?

THE CHEERLEADER FATHER

The role of a father is to steer and cheer his children to become the very best they possibly can be.

- Chris Spicer

Determining to Be a Dad
Who Encourages Others

A race of rivals fought between two of the world's oldest universities is a quintessential British sporting event simply known as "The Boat Race." Advertised as "The world's longest surviving sporting challenge," this grueling four-and-a-quarter-mile river race demands the stamina of a marathon runner and the guts of a prize fighter. Established in 1828, the Cambridge University Boat Club lives and breathes for this opportunity to beat its rival, Oxford. Crewed by amateurs, each full-time university student commits to six months of blood, sweat and tears for the chance to compete in an annual rowing race lasting about seventeen minutes.

An Oxford-educated Cambridge don named Mark de Rond spent a whole year observing the Cambridge squad and described this battle royal as: "a race marked by 'tribal rivalry,' and measured by a 'deep mutual respect'…. It is all about taking part,… yet the pain of losing is unimaginable."[1]

What might seem a strange sporting ritual to some has for

others become a not-to-be-missed pre-Easter British institution. Raced with the incoming tide of London's Thames River, each nine man crew uses slim carbon-fiber reinforced plastic racing boats known as *shells*. Of the nine crew members de Rond writes, "Eight of these are caught up in one of the most painful endurance sports imaginable for 4 miles and 374 yards on a whimsical, coffee-colored course; for rowing requires not just cardiovascular fitness but enormous will-power to be able to push oneself through successive pain barriers… until one of [the crews] decides it can no longer win."[2]

While 80 percent of the race depends on an eight man crew, the remaining 20 percent is down to choosing the right man or woman to take on the role of Cox or Coxswain. Although their value is often queried, a good Cox can make or break a team. Facing formidable waves, bitter winds and tidal influences, this is not a place for the faint-hearted. With a band of fast water barely wide enough for the two boats to run side by side without colliding, each team fights for the preferred position around three large bends in the river.

Besides various nondescript duties, the role of the Cox during the race could be brought down to two basic requirements: to *steer* and to *cheer* eight oarsmen to the finish line. As the only forward facing crew member, the Cox "has to recognize what is going wrong, why, and how it can be put right."[3] More than controlling a rudder the size of a credit card, this person has to find the fastest part of the river while negotiating a way forward that neither hinders nor helps the opposition.

Maintaining the necessary rhythm of all eight oarsmen, the Cox is required to have the spirit of a *cavalier* that makes a way for the whole "family" of oarsmen to follow in. The Cox also has the character of a *coach* that brings out the best of people. And, with his classic *cheerleader* type personality he uses diplomacy, empathy and assertion to encourage each of the crew to go all out for this one chance of winning. With a cheerleader's passion he encourages them to give their all in the pursuit of the goal. From the number one "stroke" who is setting the pace, to the "bow" man whose blade makes the most difference, the words and actions of the Cox are those best suited to coax, coach, motivate and, when necessary, calm each person as he or she strives for excellence in every stroke.

What a great illustration of the next character trait of a dad. Refusing to be passive, the *Cheerleader Father* is divinely positioned to be aware of all that is happening in and around his family. As a forward facing visionary, he is the one best placed to see the way ahead and steer each of his children through difficult waters, quickly responding to current changes. Observant of those forces working to scupper the nuclear family and sink this God-given institution in a tidal wave of liberal thinking, the cheerleader dad does whatever it takes to transition his family towards the goal. Mindful of their individual position and ability, he urges each of his children to live the moment to its fullest.

Coxing his family with empathy as well as loving assertion, the *Cheerleader Father* is constantly coaxing and coaching his children towards a perceived potential. A calming influence in challenging times, he lovingly steers and cheers on each of his kids. Boosting morale, stirring passion and dispelling fear, the *Cheerleader Father* makes every effort to encourage his kids to finish the race[4] for which they alone were born to complete.

Real Dads Do Cheer

Those who associate cheerleading with the United States as an activity almost exclusively female might be right on location but wrong in limiting it to women. Traceable back to the 1880s, cheerleading began when spectators started to organize themselves into male cheer squads to voice their support and boost the morale of a particular university. An activity originally dominated by men, cheerleading soon became an integral part of certain sporting events.

Nowadays, mention cheerleading to most guys and a picture of the pom-pom and baton carrying, brightly colored short-skirted young females will almost certainly spring to mind. Yet men like U.S. presidents (and fathers) Dwight D. Eisenhower, Franklin D. Roosevelt, Ronald Reagan and George W. Bush paid homage to the sport during their college years, showing us that real dads *do* cheer!

Although often thought of as a twentieth century phenomenon, cheerleading is traceable as far back as Bible times and is literally "as old as the hills." When God laid the foundations of the earth, the Bible tells us, "The morning stars sang in chorus and all the angels *shouted* [for joy]."[5] Could these celestial beings be the first angelic cheering squad ever?

It seems that whenever God accomplishes some awesome task, be it creation, the Incarnation of Christ, or the salvation of man, angelic beings form a celestial band of cheerleaders to celebrate another eternal win.[6] Although God desires, as well as deserves, praise and appreciation for a job well done, He certainly doesn't need the approval of others to boost His morale or motivate Him to do greater things. Yet again and again heavenly cheerleaders are seen throughout scripture celebrating major events.

Then too, the Old Testament reminds us that it was a sizeable group of cheerers who brought down the walls of Jericho,[7] while the New Testament reminds us that seated in the heavenly grandstand are those "pioneers who blazed the way," Christ followers who have died and are now viewed as venerable "veterans cheering us on."[8] Even God Himself is characterized as the eternal *Cheerleader Father* who calls for the head of every home to do the same.

When John baptized Jesus in the Jordan River, Father God praised His Son, saying, "This is my beloved son, with whom I am well pleased."[9] The epitome of true fatherhood, God also voiced words of approval and acceptance during that revelatory moment on the Mount of Transfiguration, saying, "This is my beloved Son; listen to him."[10] I see this as the divine seal of approval on the role and responsibility of the *Cheerleader Father* to be one who accepts, affirms, appreciates and thereby encourages his children.

Even the apostle Paul got in on the act. In writing to the church at Thessalonica, he said in true classic cheerleading style that he was "like a father with his child, holding your hand, *whispering encouragement*, showing you step-by-step how to live well before God, who called us into his own kingdom, into this delightful life."[11]

From an angelic cheer to a militant shout, from a venerable voice of heavenly saints to a fatherly voice of praise, encouragement, acceptance and approval, the cheerleader is played out in both the Old and New Testaments to celebrate the win, strengthen tired limbs, rouse flagging spirits and spur people on to give their all. These are basic human needs which man has the ability to *give* and *receive*. Far from being a gender issue, cheerleading is the responsibility of every guy to give out to those who call him Dad – just as a father named George did despite some challenging circumstances.

Pour It On

George was the father of Elaine, a beautiful young lady born with a severe case of Down's syndrome. With her outgoing personality, long red hair and striking blue eyes, Elaine was the joy of her father's heart. Physically deformed and having to get around with the aid of a walker, Elaine was unable to speak properly because of an oversized tongue, but to George she was a beautiful princess. Perceived as having an incredible inner and outer beauty, this young lady was left with no doubt of her father's unconditional love. George had the ability to see beyond the physical, mental and emotional disability into the untapped possibility of Elaine's young life.

Whenever George entered the room, Elaine's eyes would light up. As she squealed with joy at the sight of her dad, he would sweep her up in his arms and hold her deformed face in his hands. Cheering her on to believe in herself, his words of approval were always framed in the same all-embracing statements, "I love you, Elaine. You are beautiful. And God loves you, Elaine." Sealing his love and acceptance with a kiss on the forehead, even on the dreariest of days Elaine was left basking in the sunlight of a father's love—a daughter loved for who she was and not what she could or couldn't do.

A strong-willed, stubborn and determined young lady, some found Elaine difficult to handle, yet, when her father walked into the room a world of possibilities opened up to her. Always the divine optimist, George was by nature a man who chose to see the good in others, to value people rather than horde things, to build up rather than tear down, and sacrificially give of himself for the sake of others. George was the classic *Cheerleader Father* who sought through all means possible to bring the best out of his children. While the physical, emotional and mental challenges tried to dampen his daughter's spirit, George continually filled her with victory, encouragement, acceptance and appreciation.

It doesn't take a genius to realize that the world—and many families—are suffering from a psychological pandemic. Dehydrated of praise, their spirits dragging, thousands of people are seeking someone or something to pour love and approval into their sad and empty lives. Statistics bear witness to that.

One United States government agency says that each year 1.6

million young people either run away or are sent away from home. To this shocking statistic they add that around 200,000 children are on the streets of America at any given time; of these, 5,000 will die from assault, illness or suicide.[12] Similarly, more than 100,000 children in the United Kingdom run away from home every year, twice as many as previously estimated. Most of these runaways are trying to escape the carnage of what might loosely be called *home*. Having suffered physical or mental abuse (or both) and the lack of basic childcare, these children find themselves sleeping in derelict buildings, fields and even graveyards.[13]

Unlike the happy ending to the biblical story of the prodigal son,[14] most of these kids don't have a father waiting at home ready to receive them back with open arms. Lacking the kind of father figure who pours love and acceptance into their lives no matter what they've said or done, many of these young people left home in the first place because their fathers provoked them to leave. The fact is our children need to know that, regardless of how bad things get, we will always be their number-one cheerleader.

Bring Out the Best, Not the Beast

The apostle Paul wrote in a letter to the Ephesians some timeless advice for all fathers: "Do not irritate and provoke your children to anger [do not exasperate them to resentment]."[15] Although Paul was Jewish, he was raised in a Roman culture, so it's almost certain that he was acutely aware of the cruel way in which some fathers treated their children. Rather than the self-controlled, gentle, patient and encouraging educators he outlines in his letter to Christian fathers residing in Ephesus, his own upbringing may have been quite different.

As the head of the family, Roman fathers would exercise their autocratic right to punish, kill or dispose of their children as they alone saw fit. Exercising absolute power, a father could sell his children into slavery or make them work in fields in chains. Because Roman fathers had the last word on any matter, they acted as prosecutor, judge and jury, and, by taking the law into their own hands, they became the exact opposite of what Paul was exhorting Christian fathers to be.

Perhaps Paul harbored some ill feelings toward his own religious upbringing. Maybe his father made unrealistic demands on him or found fault in his son's behavior when he refused to apply himself to the requirements of traditional orthodoxy. Whatever the truth, the reality is that Paul in scripture urged fathers not to *irritate, exasperate, provoke, stir up, discourage, embitter* and *dishearten* their children through hurtful words, inconsistency, hypocrisy, unrealistic demands, distrust, faultfinding, partiality and neglect. That kind of parental behavior will eventually break the spirit of our children and open the door to negative influences.[16]

We live in a world that is fast becoming overcrowded with broken-spirited children. Despite his divinely delegated authority to shape his kids' lives to be their best, the damaging words of a dolt dad can result in a child becoming "discouraged,"[17] disengaged, deprived and even depressed. Consequently, he or she is robbed of that drive, enthusiasm and spirited nature necessary to accomplish great things. The loss of such passion for life is often the result of overbearing fathers who, knowingly or unknowingly, dismiss their children's dreams or burst their bubble. Rather than harness their kids' nature to be builders, pioneers, entrepreneurs, inventors, out-of-the-box-thinkers, for instance, these fathers break the zeal of potentially adventurous people who are needed so badly in this world.

Using negative instead of positive provocation, these deadbeat dads tend to bring out the *beast* rather than the *best* in their children. Paul felt so strongly about this that his letter to the Colossians was similar to what he had written to the Ephesians: "Fathers, do not provoke or irritate or fret your children [do not be hard on them or harass them], lest they become discouraged and sullen and morose and feel inferior and frustrated. [*Do not break their spirit.*]"[18]

When our child places a small hand in ours, it may be smeared in chocolate, sticky with ice cream or dirty from stroking the dog or playing in the mud; but it's the hand that some day may hold a Bible or a gun, may play an instrument or mess with drugs, dress the wounds of a leper or shake uncontrollably with the effects of alcohol. Right now their hand is in ours, looking to us to help and guide them, and we must not let them down.

As a recognizer of potential, an encourager of effort, a booster of morale, a sounder of praise, a beater of the drum, each dad is called to be his children's number-one fan. The word *encouragement* often paints a picture of someone called alongside to help those in time of need. A *Cheerleader Dad* can come alongside his child, give of himself to strengthen, to jump-start a stalled life if necessary, and provoke that young person (in a positive way) to accomplish great things.

The Encouragement Connection

Suppose it's a sub-zero January morning and you're late for an appointment. You step into your only means of transport, turn the key to start your vehicle and...nothing. From the horrible whirring noise coming from the engine compartment every time you turn the key, you realize that your battery is "flat" or "dead." The reality is you're stalled and going nowhere. All the potential encapsulated in that four-wheeled vehicle is of little value. What's needed is a friend, someone willing to take the time to bring their vehicle alongside yours, make a good power source connection, jump-start your vehicle and get you on the way to your desired destination.

Whether through general neglect or excessive use, people, like batteries, can become drained of energy, zeal and enthusiasm. Although still going through the motions of daily life, they're mentally, physically or spiritually stalled and heading nowhere. Worn down by other people, objects and events, their stationary lives need an infusion of encouragement to get them going again. A doctor named Luke wrote of a classic example in the New Testament.

In the story of the disciples who were walking on the Emmaus Road,[19] we see two men who were discouraged and disillusioned by the recent death of Jesus Christ on the cross. Both of these disciples may have been going through the physical motions of walking the familiar road between Jerusalem and Emmaus, but spiritually and emotionally they were stalled so badly that it took the risen Christ taking the time to draw alongside and make a conversational connection to get them going. By giving of Himself, Jesus fired up this discouraged duo to such an extent that they retraced their steps and journeyed the seven miles back to Jerusalem in order to spark others with the same encouragement they had experienced from Him.

Encouragement is a means to strengthen the emotional makeup of someone, as Jesus did that day. Likewise, it is a basic ingredient to being a *Cheerleader Father.* To make an encouragement connection with his kids means reviving a stalled life, like jump-starting a vehicle, and it requires willingness to do certain things.

Take the time —
The kind friend helping you out on that cold January morning has to be willing to accept a detour, to become distracted from other pursuits, and suffer personal inconvenience in order to meet your needs rather than his own. Similarly, to creatively and constructively "cheerlead" his children requires a father sacrificing a good measure of a commodity that in these days is often in short supply — *time.*

I've observed that, no matter how crazy the daily schedule is of the *Cheerleader Father*, he somehow manages to give each of his children a fair share (quantity and quality) of time. His presence is a provocation that seeks to steer and cheer his children in the right direction.

With or without words, the willingness of *Cheerleader Dads* to take time to simply be there speaks volumes to their kids. Their love is undaunted, their commitment unquestioned, and their encouragement is unending, for these are the makers and menders of young lives, fathers who mold a future generation with words of approval, affirmation and appreciation. Dads like this see the untapped possibilities in their kids and give them the confidence they need to succeed at whatever they put their hand to in life.

Come alongside —

When the ancient Greeks spoke of encouragement, they often used a word that described military reinforcement arriving at the heat of battle to help a beleaguered army.[20] In modern times, the American forces "encouraged" their European allies when joining the fight to defeat Hitler in World War II. Both are symbolic of the *Cheerleader Father* drawing alongside his children to boost their flagging morale and motivate potential losers in such a way as to turn them into celebrated winners. True encouragement is more than great words or gifted resources — it ultimately requires the visible personal presence of the encourager.

As we all know by experience, it's possible to be physically present, while mentally absent. A child knows intuitively when his or her father is bodily present but subconsciously somewhere else. Partial hearing, head-nodding syndrome, earth-to-father stuff — none of these cut it when it comes to making a good connection with our kids.

Coming alongside them with a timely hug, a listening ear, an empathetic look, or a loving smile are all measures of the silent approval that an encourager uses to make his presence known. To act creatively, to listen empathetically, to talk encouragingly and write spontaneously are the means by which we let our children know we love them unconditionally.

Make a connection —

In a society where kids are tuned in and connected to everything technical from iPods to cell phones, the one connection they all need is with their dads. We've seen that mothers bond with their children right from the start, but it's a work in progress for fathers. Some dads never make the connection and their kids are left struggling to survive with an emptiness from the lack of their father's encouragement and approval.

Greg Norman, reckoned to be one of the most ice-cold golfers on the circuit, learned his chilling demeanor from his father. For most of his adult life, Greg and his dad were not close. After long periods of separation, when both men would meet up Greg would often think, *Wouldn't it be great to give my dad a big hug? God, wouldn't that be great?* Then he would remember, *My dad's not like that,* and both men would shake hands.[21] Cracks in Norman's icy exterior began to appear during the closing moments of the 1996 Master's golf tournament.

In what has been called the "Agony at Augusta," Norman watched as a six-shot lead slipped away during the final holes of the championship. Eventually losing the prestigious Green Jacket to Nick Faldo's 15-foot birdie putt, Greg was devastated. In an effort to console him and offer his condolence on his loss, Nick walked over to offer what Norman thought would be a few kind words and a standard congratulatory handshake.

To Norman's shock, he found himself in a bear hug embrace, and while they held each other he began to weep. Most people thought his tears were the result of his devastating defeat, but he later explained, "I wasn't crying because I'd lost.... I've lost a lot of golf tournaments. I'll lose a lot more. I cried because I'd never felt that from another man before. I've never had a hug like that in my life."[22]

Disconnected fathers produce disconnected children. It takes time and effort to find the frequency our kids are on, to tune in to their perspective, which may or may not be wrong, just different. To make the connection with them requires discovering what they think, feel, value, love, hate, fear, desire, hope for, believe in and are committed to. Positive connectivity brings the best out of kids.

Michael Ray King, author and father of six, doesn't mince words about this: "It is not enough to tell your children 'good job' and 'good night.' Quick surface oriented communication is not what drives the desires of your children. As a father, you can't come home from work and plop down in front of the television with your children and call that interaction.... If you limit yourself to cursory conversations stolen during station breaks, all you will have to show for your time and effort later in life is a distant, detached relationship with your son or daughter."[23]

Give of yourself —
The New Testament woman whose life had been stalled for twelve years through illness found energizing life when she connected with Jesus and touched the hem of his garment. He, in turn, felt that "power had gone out from him."[24] The bottom line is that the discouraged can draw from an encourager when the encourager willingly gives of their time, energy, effort and resources to help others.

The giving of oneself, for me (an imperfect father), has been one of the most challenging aspects of fatherhood. As a self-centered teenager who carried his "me mentality" into the realms of marriage and fatherhood, I know what it's like to hold on to time, energy and resources, rather than pouring them unselfishly on my children. Sometimes it would be easier to give gifts than oneself, and even now I cringe when thinking of those times when my kids needed a hug and I gave them hollow words; those moments they needed a father and I gave them a pastor; the times when they needed my appearance and I gave apologies.

The absence of a cheerleader has a debilitating affect on the ongoing development of children, which they often carry into their adult years, an issue recently highlighted in the case of a young man called John.[25] Seeking to come to terms with the recent death of his non-cheerleading father, John was stalled. Needing to make the encouragement connection, a Christian counselor took time to draw alongside and suggested John write an imaginary letter from his father — the kind of letter John would have loved to discover when going through his deceased father's personal papers. Here is what John wrote:

Dear John,

I'm so sorry for all the things I was not there for, the lost opportunities of spending time together. I wish I was there, on those days you came home from school and needed to talk about how you were mistreated and the names they called you. I wish I was there to tell you that you're just as good as anyone else. I wish I was there, when you needed encouragement and comfort. I wish I was there, to tell you just how smart you are and not to listen to what others say. I wish I was there, to go to all those concerts and shows you were in and tell you what a great job you did and how proud I was of you. And when I did go, I wish I had shown you more enthusiasm. I just wish I was there for you more, so we could spend time together, to go to a ball game, a movie, and talk about things that were going on in each of our lives. I just can't tell you how sorry I am and how much — I just wish I was there.

I love you John,
Dad

This writing exercise enabled John to express his deep-seated emotions concerning the loss of a father who reneged on his commitment. It was a process of forgiveness that allowed John to bring closure to a painful chapter in his life and move on towards his God-given destiny. A father figure (the Christian counselor) made this possible by simply being willing *to take the time, come alongside, make the connection,* and *give of his time, energy and resources* to jump-start a stalled life.

You may not be a divine optimist by nature or have a counseling degree, but you can make an effort to speak words of encouragement to your children whenever the opportunity arises. Sure, there'll be times when you don't feel like it or it's not convenient, but the benefits outweigh the alternatives. Indifference inhibits, anger devastates, abuse breaks, flattery manipulates; but your encouragement and praise minister to your kids' inner well-being and lets them know that you accept them for who they are rather than what they do. That brings out the best in any child.

A life influenced by a *Cheerleader Dad* receives vision, motivation and wise counsel from a father (or father figure, like a friend or family member) and is encouraged to reach their full potential. Denzel Washington, award-winning actor and national spokesperson for Boys and Girls Clubs of America, is convinced that each individual success is rooted in that kind of positive inspiration: "I don't care who you are or what you do for a living," he says, "if you do it well I'm betting there was someone cheering you on and showing you the way."[26]

Personal Reflections

• Describe in your own words how you would characterize the *Cheerleader Father*.

• List the name of someone who has been your greatest cheerleader.

• Name one thing your cheerleader did to make you feel accepted, approved and appreciated.

• On a scale of 1–10 (one being extremely poor and ten excellent) where do you place yourself in the cheerleading department?

• Think of each of your children in turn and begin to list some of the things you know that they *value, love, hate, fear, desire, hope for, believe in* and are *committed to*.

• Now begin to think creatively as to how you have in the past or how you intend in the future to encourage them in some of these areas.

 ## Group Discussion

Get together with a small group of fathers and begin to share how you are planning to find the time to draw alongside each of your children so as to make a strong connection and give of your time, energy and resources to bring out the best in each of them.

THE COMPASS FATHER

Fathers, don't exasperate your children...[but] take them by the hand and lead them in the way of the Master.

- Ephesians 6:4 MSG

Determining to Be a Dad
Who Gives Good Direction

O f the 70 million people who pass through Chicago O' Hare Airport every year, probably not many know that a father/son relationship indirectly led to the naming of America's second busiest airport.

Chicago was at one time a city virtually owned by the notorious gangster Al Capone. Making his fortune from numerous unsavory activities, "Scarface" managed to maintain his lucrative criminal empire by relying on the legal maneuverings of his lawyer, Edgar Joseph O'Hare. It was his skill that kept Capone out of jail, and for services rendered he became a lawyer who lived well on his ill-gotten gains. Residing in a mansion and grounds big enough to fill an entire city block, the man known as "Easy Eddie" seemingly had everything money could buy— except for one thing.

Although hardened by years of criminal activity, Eddie had a soft spot for his son, Butch. In monetary terms Butch wanted for nothing, but his father was desperate to leave him a legacy of which he would be proud. To possess moral values, to invest in integrity, and serve others without thought of personal gain were all things Easy Eddie wanted desperately to pass on to Butch.

In order to guide his son in the right direction, Eddie took some drastic steps to rectify his previous misdemeanors. Turning state's evidence, it was his information that allowed the authorities to jail Al Capone for tax evasion, a choice that probably cost Butch's dad his life. Gunned down in a gangland style murder, Eddie's 180 degree decision may have been the turning point that forever changed his family's fortunes. Not that Chicago's O'Hare International Airport is named after the somewhat dubious activities of "Easy Eddie," but rather the heroic acts of his son—World War II fighter pilot Lt. Com. Edward Henry "Butch" O'Hare.

Assigned to protect the aircraft carrier USS Lexington, Lt. Com. O'Hare had been sent on a mission with other Wildcat fighters to intercept nine incoming Japanese bombers. Along with his wingman, Butch was the first to spot the planes. While the rest of the Wildcats were too far away to be of any assistance, the two pilots decided to engage the enemy alone. However, O'Hare's wingman's gun jammed leaving him no option but to go it alone.

Without a moment's hesitation, Butch flew his plane at full throttle into the V formation of oncoming Japanese bombers in what his citation later read as, "One of the most daring, if not the most daring, single action in the history of aviation." Downing five enemy planes and damaging another, Lt. Com. O'Hare displayed a level of personal sacrifice, honor and gallantry that earned him the Congressional Medal of Honor and the respect of a whole nation.

Butch O'Hare took his bearings from a father who seemingly tried to redirect his own misguided life so as to point his son in the right direction. Edgar O'Hare's task of "compassing" changed the course of his son's life.

Being a dad is more than mowing the lawn, paying bills, taking out the trash, kicking a ball, or monopolizing the remote. Yet, exactly how does an imperfect father direct his children, while at the same time valuing their growing desire to make choices? How do we govern, as well as guide, and lead those we love without their losing sight of their unique reason for being? I believe the answer lies in a dad's ability to "compass" his kids in the right direction.

Fixed Point of Reference

Much like the instrument from which he gets his name, the *Compass Father* has the inherent ability to give each of his children godly direction by being a standard from whom others can take a reliable bearing. In an ever-changing world, children need solid benchmarks from which they can take a bearing in all things moral, social, emotional and spiritual. The consistency of the *Compass Father* is the fixed point of reference that enables his kids to take those reliable readings — an ability that, although humanly inherent, is most certainly divinely inspired.

Becoming a dad for the first time can make a man feel ill-prepared, ill-informed, ill-equipped and ill-suited for the task that childbirth springs on him. With the arrival of a new baby, life takes on a more serious and reflective nature. When an Old Testament pensioner named Enoch fathered his firstborn, the Bible is quick to tell us that he "walked with God."[1] The miracle of birth awakens a man to the reality that he needs the daily companionship of Father/God.

In his foreword for a book on fatherhood, Rabbi Harold Kushner described what fatherhood means to a dad: "To father a child is, in a way, to partake of the divine, to bring a new soul into the world even as God did in the first days of Creation, to cheat mortality by seeing to it that your name and your values, as well as your DNA, will survive your limited time on earth."[2] Yet, it leaves most men feeling vulnerable.

Our children's birth awakens us to the reality that in order to give directions we first must take directions, that as fathers we too need a fixed point of reference in our own lives, something or someone we can trust to be reliable, no matter what is going on around us. A defining moment in a man's life, fatherhood is an "Enoch Experience" that should birth a sincere desire to have God join us on our daily journey into parenting.

As "the Father of lights, with whom there is no variation or shadow due to change,"[3] God alone is the fixed point of reference we can trust, no matter how difficult the terrain or how bad the environment. While new birth might awaken us to our own mortality, it also opens our eyes to the need for spiritual intimacy, to enter into and enjoy a relationship with God the Father,[4] whose directional advice for dads is invaluable in what is, undoubtedly, the world's most difficult job.

Society doesn't need more fathers whose parenting job description is "do as I say, not as I do," dads who merely point in a certain direction and expect their children to magically obey their orders. We need guys who will lovingly take their children by the hand and lead them in the ways of God.

Just two days into the Apollo 13 mission and about 200,000 miles from earth, the vessel's number two oxygen tank exploded, ripping a hole in the service module, threatening the survival of the whole crew. That's when the Apollo 13 commander Jim Lovell uttered those five infamous words: "Houston, we've had a problem."[5] The thought of losing an American anywhere in the world was unacceptable; losing one in space was inconceivable. While the successful mission to recover those astronauts was a credit to human endurance and man's ingenuity in the face of appalling odds, Western civilization is now facing a far greater crisis.

A post-Christian culture has removed the fixed points of reference, the benchmarks by which the founding fathers established our civilization, leaving us a generation lost in its own uncertainty. So how do we retrieve a generation lost through the destructive force of liberal thinking?

Ask a parent to describe the flood of emotion that sweeps over them when they first realize they've lost track of their child in a busy store and few will be able to adequately explain the feelings of unadulterated panic, followed by guilt, fear and anger. With emotions off the chart, horror soon turns to hysteria as a volcanic voice begins to erupt deep inside that wants so desperately to cry out, "Close the doors! Don't let anyone leave! I've lost my child."

If there was ever a moment in history when children need to catch sight of a fixed point of reference, it's now; but in a world without signposts, Western civilization is fast losing track of its most valuable "commodity" — its children

Putting Back the Signposts

As the European nations fell like dominoes under the might of the German war machine, England braced itself for invasion. World War II was at its height and Great Britain feared the worst. In a defensive move aimed at eradicating all forms of navigational advantage to an invading army, the government of the day ordered that all road signs be removed. Because they provided such vital pieces of information as destination, direction and distance of local towns and cities throughout the United Kingdom, the order was to dismantle all the signposts for the duration of the war. Removing these directional signs, the government hoped to significantly slow Hitler's progress during the early days of his threatened occupation.

By divorcing from the Judeo-Christian belief system, modern man has removed the signposts that are the navigational markers of *absolute truth, ethical right, delegated authority, long-term commitment, ownership* and *personal morality*. Confused by the mixture of syncretism, the maze of relativism and the madness of pluralism, a post-Christian culture has exploded in the face of our children, leaving the twenty-first century fumbling to find its way in a fog of varying beliefs.

As a result of breaking free from biblical absolutes, mankind has created a perfect storm in which their offspring find themselves floating directionless in a sea of adolescence. Sailing rudderless, young people lack the necessary steering mechanism to cope with the winds of change and avoid either the shallows or those submerged obstacles that threaten to run them aground or shipwreck their lives. Tossed about by the winds of change and the waves of adversity, adults and adolescents alike are being shipwrecked on the shores of physical, emotional, financial and spiritual ruin at a rate that is fast outstripping our human resources.

In the aftermath of the sixties, Western humanity ran amuck in the candy store of liberal thinking. Momentarily enjoying a sugar-rush of freedom, the West thought itself free of those moral moorings imposed on them by previous generations. Yet, although liberal thinkers would argue otherwise, humanity needs signposts, fixed points of reference from which an emerging generation can find their bearings and recalibrate their belief system to the benchmark of biblical truth.

No matter how challenging the crisis, the way back for civilization is in the hands of *Compassing Fathers* — those who are willing to monitor and model the borders and boundaries and become major players in their children's directional journey in life.

Drawing a "Line in the Sand"

Children seem to always test the borders and boundaries to see if their parents' will-power is still plugged in sufficiently to say no. All kids need parameters, directives, perspective and horizons — borders and boundaries — that will both govern and guide them. Psychologists and boundary experts Henry Cloud and John Townsend wonderfully described it in their book *Boundaries*: "Just as homeowners set physical property lines around their land, we need to set mental, physical, emotional, and spiritual boundaries for our lives to help us distinguish what is our responsibility and what is not. The inability to set appropriate boundaries at appropriate times with the appropriate people can be very destructive."[6]

In a later publication called *Boundaries with Kids*, the two authors noted that "adults with boundary problems had not developed those problems as grown-ups. They had learned patterns early in life and then continued those out-of-control patterns in their adult lives, where the stakes were higher."[7] To avoid this happening in our own children's lives, our responsibility as fathers is two-fold: to set *borders* our kids are encouraged to reach out to, and to establish the *boundaries* they should not cross or try to remove.

When the children of Israel first entered the Promised Land, God had them subdivide the territory into tribal lots. In the process, families would set up markers, property lines, landmarks that would identify what was legally theirs and which no one was permitted to remove.[8] These *borders* clearly defined the extent that each family member was encouraged to "reach to."[9]

Imagine Jewish fathers periodically walking the property line with their children, pointing out the landmarks in order to inspire them to go the distance, to reach for everything that was within their grasp and reap the benefits from all that God had made available to them. This act of compassing is no less important today. The modern-day *Compass Father* lovingly exercises his divinely delegated authority ultimately to release and not restrict his children. He points out the borders of personal possibility beckoning to them to break free from small-mindedness and progressively reach out to the furthest extent of their individual potential in life.[10]

While the "landmarks" *inspire* our children, "lines in the sand" will *instruct* them. Show me a child who learned to accept boundaries and I'll show you an adult who is able to handle responsibility, liberty and authority. When we allow the winds of change to obliterate the behavioral lines in the sand, we give our children permission to run free in the candy store. And while today's obnoxious behavior in a young child might seem humorous to some, the same liberty to say and do as we please as adults is horrific.

Children need to understand that no means no[11] and that living life with borders and boundaries is important. This is a basic ingredient of the *Compass Father* – to verbally and visually demonstrate what is and isn't acceptable behavior (by establishing fixed points of reference). If, as so often happens, a child stops reaching out to the borders of their personal potential or oversteps those parental boundaries, the *Compass Father* lovingly seeks to either inspire or instruct his children to help them recalibrate their inner compass.

The task of compassing is wonderful in theory; it's the practice we find challenging! How does an imperfect father bring challenge and correction while appreciating his children's growing ability to make their own choices? To monitor a child's direction while allowing his or her own unique personality to be developed is extremely difficult. Yet a small adjustment now can save them from those major adjustments later in life. For instance, lack of respect, loss of self-control, and the inability to listen or follow through on a given task presently might seem insignificant, but the absence of such things in later life will prove disastrous.

When children lack a fixed point of reference, they struggle. They need a road map to guide them through uncharted territory, and someone who can help them to know how and when to engage such emotions as love, desire, hate, anger and passion; how and when to face issues of purity, honesty, integrity and fairness; how and when to engage or disengage people, objects and events in a godly way.

Take sex, for example. The reason why sex has become a moral dilemma among so many young people is that parents have not instructed them in how to handle the power and potential of this God-given gift. Leaving our children prey to movies, magazines, the Internet and misinformed friends is not how they should find their way through the moral maze of all things sexual. Some mothers wrongly teach their daughters that sex is a moral duty they have to perform, while a number of fathers somehow convey a warped view of the opposite sex. Godly parents should help their children not only celebrate their sexuality, but understand the biblical basis for enjoyable sex within the confines (or borders and boundaries) of the marriage vow between a man and a woman.

We all possess an inner compass, a conscience, a God-given early warning system that enables us to make choices. Dulled and deadened by man's continual disobedience, each of us needs to have our system recalibrated by surrendering our lives to God's Son Jesus. Asking for His forgiveness will bring about a faith-encounter that not only regenerates our spiritually dead state, but realigns our inner compass and resensitizes us to His ways.

When God Goes Walkabout

During adolescence, Australian Aboriginal men undergo a journey commonly known as *Walkabout*. It's a period of time when they live in the wilderness so as to learn the ways of their forefathers. Although folklore can trace these rituals back thousands of years, the Judeo-Christian God was going "Walkabout" with His kids long before the Aborigines.

At the dawn of history, the Old Testament patriarch Enoch went on a Walkabout with his heavenly Father that lasted at least 300 years.[12] But, perhaps the most famous biblical Walkabout of all time was the forty-year journey God undertook with the nation of Israel. Like a father guides his kids,[13] Jehovah journeyed the children of Israel from the POW camps of Egypt to the Promised Land of Canaan. As a rite of passage from slavery to sonship, God took the opportunity to "discipline" or "instruct"[14] His children to enable them to reach their full potential in life.

Although seldom mentioned in the Old Testament,[15] the fatherhood of God is clearly seen in His relationship with the nation of Israel.[16] Transitioning His children from who they were to who they would yet become, the New Testament reminds us that "these things happened to them as an example, [and... are] written down for our instruction."[17] The wilderness experience illustrates God's way for fathers to compass our children towards their destiny in life: *personally*, *lovingly* and *redemptively*.

Personally.

Personal involvement is imperative in this age of electronic surrogacy. The average British child spends around five hours a day watching television, playing computer games or surfing the Internet. Those things aren't any better in America, for "adolescent boys (7–12 grade) are using electronic media the same amount as they would be working a full time job (44.5 hours a week, 6.5 hours every day)."[18]

The statistics are scary, and one might be tempted to ask, "Whatever happened to interpersonal relationships in which parents spend time communicating face to face with their kids?" The fact is Facebook, MySpace, Twitter, texting and various forms of instant messaging have the potential to produce a generation that, although technically skilled, is socially inept.

When young people are more likely to relationally connect through one of those technologies than face to face, we have not only dehumanized true community, we have undermined personal relationships. As Life Coach David Bartholomew warns,

"Many of the activities boys engage in today don't contribute to social skills, personal interaction, work ethic, motivation or future success. For hours and hours a day, boys are well entertained, but they are not well trained for life."[19]

The *wilderness* environment in which God chose to go Walkabout with His children comes from a Hebrew word that means "mouth" or "speech."[20] Basically, it could be translated as an ongoing conversation. Rather than parenting by proxy, God the Father got up close and personal with His kids, as together they embarked on a forty-year "conversation" aimed at changing their beliefs and their behavior, and ultimately what they would become in this world.

Although being a "distant dad" is for some unavoidable, when Father/God took His children on that conversational camping trip lasting forty years He as good as said, "If you're going to live in tents, I want you to build Me a tent, so I can be where you are and journey with you personally."[21] None of this "kids in a tent, dad in a hotel" stuff; Father/God made Himself accessible and became purposely involved in His children's everyday lives, so as to guide them to their destiny.

When we as fathers inadvertently allow people, objects and events to guide our children, we take our hands off the tiller and leave them to the mercy of the prevailing wind that will eventually run them aground or shipwreck them.

Lovingly.
When God went Walkabout with His children, He showed

incredible *loving-kindness* and commitment to a group of kids who, at times, were the most rude, unruly and disrespectful bunch of "brats" you could ever have the misfortune to parent. Yet, refusing to renege on His commitment,[22] Father/God exercised a covenant love, a strong binding agreement that tied Him in to the task of bringing the best out of them no matter what. As someone once said, "Becoming a dad is a bit like becoming a monk. It takes a lot of devotion."[23]

Throughout the wilderness experience, God enveloped His children in what the Bible calls "lovingkindness,"[24] a demonstrative love that's willing to do whatever it takes to provide life's basic needs[25] and protect from destructive forces.[26] It's the kind of love the apostle Paul describes in his letter to the church at Corinth.

Love never gives up. Love cares more for others than for self. Love doesn't want what it doesn't have. Love doesn't strut, doesn't have a swelled head, doesn't force itself on others, isn't always "me first," doesn't fly off the handle, doesn't keep score of the sins of others, doesn't revel when others grovel, takes pleasure in the flowering of truth, puts up with anything, trusts God always, always looks for the best, never looks back, but keeps going to the end.[27]

Obviously what Paul talked about here is not a natural love common to man. It's unconditional love that we can't help but exhibit when we have a relationship with our heavenly Father, for as the apostle John told us, "God is love."[28]

Redemptively.

Everything Father/God did during His conversational Walkabout with the children of Israel revolved around a *redemptive attitude*. His intent was to buy back what had been lost to Egyptian thinking and enable His kids to become all He had in mind for them to be. Counteracting years of Egyptian culture, the Father compassed his children toward their predetermined destiny. Beginning with a redemptive act to get them out of Egypt, God parented His children in such a way as to get Egypt out of them, an exercise that at times made Him unpopular.

Nowadays, for fathers to get "Egypt" out of their kids means to get worldly ways and ideals out of them. Maybe this is what Paul was referring to when he wrote, "Have you forgotten how good parents treat children, and that God regards you as his children?... God is educating you; that's why you must never drop out. He's treating you as dear children. This trouble you're in isn't punishment; it's training, the normal experience of children. Only irresponsible parents leave children to fend for themselves.... We respect our own parents for training and not spoiling us, so why not embrace God's training so we can truly live?"[29]

For a loving parent to make small compass corrections to a child's behavior now is far better than having other people trying to make major adjustments in the future.

When parents choose popularity over principle, problems soon begin to emerge. Compassing a child involves directing and correcting on a chosen route. Through his *personal involvement*, *loving-kindness* and *redemptive attitude*, a *Compass Father* directs his children towards "True North," saving them from themselves and a secular culture set on warping their young minds.

God's True North

I have taught for many years in Bible colleges and local churches. When starting a new course on the subject of *Attitudes*, I will normally ask the class to join me in a simple exercise. Having everyone stand, I ask that they close their eyes and, on the count of three, point to what they believe is north. Generally all points of the globe are covered by people whose fingers are aimed toward every conceivable direction of the compass. One "directionally challenged" person's finger invariably points to the ceiling, much to the amusement of the class members who by now are seeing the various opinions as to which direction is north. At this moment in the exercise we consult a compass and congratulate those whose sense of direction is proven correct.

Without a compass, there could never be an agreement on who was right, for if we are to truly know what is north we need a fixed point of reference. To date, no one in my classes has asked if I required *Magnetic North* or *True North*, but there is a difference. The Magnetic North is not at the North Pole, the absolute geographic northern spot on this planet. The fact is, while the compass points to Magnetic North, if we were to follow it to its ultimate northern point we would be 1,500 miles away from absolute north or True North. Navigators have to make constant adjustments so as to align themselves to True North and arrive safely at their preferred destination. In terms of fathering, then, the question has to be, "Which north are we heading for?"

While all humans have an inner compass that gives them some sense of moral right, that compass by its very nature needs to be recalibrated to God's True North. As the biblical proverb reads, "There is a way that seems right to a man"[30] but the end result is disastrous. By reason of our fallen nature (since Adam and Eve fell in the garden), we are, naturally speaking, in constant danger of missing the mark because "all have sinned and fall short [and miss the mark]"[31] of what God intended for humanity. Like an arrow falling short of its intended target, mankind has this inbuilt misalignment (a bias the Bible calls *sin*) that causes us to deviate from God's absolute Truth North.

If our inner compass is not aligned with God's True North, then we are all in constant danger of missing the desired destination He has for us. Jesus Christ did not come to tell us about a way but rather to tell us that He is *"the way,* and the truth, and the life," and that "No one comes to the Father except through me."[32] Therefore, as fathers we may be consciously or subconsciously teaching our children a way of life that our fathers taught us, but the question is, "Is it a Magnetic North or a biblical True North?"

In his book *Born Again,* Charles Colson, one of former President Richard Nixon's closest aides, gives us an inside view of the White House during one of the greatest government scandals in American history. Dedicating his book to his father, Wendell Colson, Charles writes: "To my Dad—whose ideals for my life I have tried, not always successfully, to fulfill—and whose strength and support is with me today."[33] Chuck, as his father preferred to call him, sought to align himself to his father's core values, a man he once described as "the straightest of straight arrows."[34] Although Chuck took a wrong turn during the Nixon administration, he refers to the compass-like character of his father as a reference point from which he could take a bearing and find a moral True North.

Sailing a sailboat is one form of navigation that involves bearing taking and finding True North. To enjoy the experience and arrive at a predetermined destination, you must first pick a fixed point of reference on the distant shore and steer towards it, no matter what. Always watching out for submerged obstacles, shallow water and bad weather, a good sailor knows that to be blown off course is expected, but to run aground isn't. I've found that fatherhood is a lot like sailing a sailboat. To arrive at a predetermined destination, fathers, like sailors, accept and expect to have to periodically make minor adjustments. And both need to have a specific course planned at the onset of their journey so they are assured of going in the right direction.

Aaron, a young pastor friend of mine, is willing to do whatever it takes to point his four young children in the right direction. Believing that a dad's role is to show his children how to live the Christian life, Aaron wants to compass all of his youngsters through their formative years. So he and his wife, Sarah, have devised a plan consisting of three one-year personal development programs.

"There are key development years in our kids' lives," he wrote to me recently, "like the year before junior high when our kids are in 5th grade [*10-11 years of age*], 9th grade [*15 years of age*] and then their last year of high school. Knowing this and the difficulty and the challenges that are often associated with these transitional years, we've prepared a twelve-month-long discipleship program for each of them."

Beginning with a camping trip to discuss the coming year, their program includes such things as: Dad going out for breakfast and taking walks with each of his children to engage in meaningful conversations; a planned reading program that includes the Bible and other books, such as a modern version of *Pilgrim's Progress*; serving the poor and marginalized; as well as shadowing their father in memorizing the Sermon on the Mount.[35] This is a learning program that Aaron feels will not only change his children but challenge him, because he knows that there are no perfect dads or moms.

"We fail many times as parents because we don't ask our kids the right questions and then stop and listen to the answers," he said. "I believe our kids understand and are more sensitive than we give them credit."

Whether through not taking time to talk *and* listen to our kids, or through personal insecurity, ignorance, independence or some other integral inability to lead, many fathers seem to struggle when it comes to helping their children throw away ballast, trim their sails, turn a rudder and make small compass adjustments. Floating directionless in a sea of adolescence, children need the

Compass Father to guide them through the storms, submerged obstacles, adverse winds and crosscurrents of everyday life. They need dads who will direct them without the excuses of time, temperament or tiredness.

If there is one gift a father can give his children, it is the ability to make good choices and follow a right direction in life. Maybe that's why a father called Hermann gave his five-year-old son a compass. Whatever his reason, "this simple instrument completely fascinated the youth, who couldn't understand why the needles always pointed north...there must be a mysterious invisible force that acted on the compass needle causing it to hold its position,"[36] reasoned the young Albert Einstein.

With God's help the *Compass Father* can hold his position of godly vision and values for his children and direct their lives to embrace a positive attitude, a disciplined lifestyle, a willingness to serve others and a determination to never quit, no matter what. To compass them so they desire to follow a way of integrity, honesty, morality, fairness, consistency and spirituality that will become a fixed point of reference is a gift that will last them a lifetime.

Personal Reflections

• Did the lack of a *Compass Father* in any way affect your young life and, if so, how do you intend to avoid that with your children?

• Have you allowed any spiritual signposts to be removed from your own family, and how do you intend to reinstate them?

• Knowing each of your children as you do, what are the borders you intend to inspire them to reach?

• Can you describe the boundaries you have set for each of your children and how you intend to manage them in a loving way?

• Do you feel that you are personally, lovingly and redemptively journeying with each of your children in a conversational "Walkabout" that is progressing them toward their destiny?

 ## Group Discussion

Think about what it was like becoming a father for the first time, and the sobering affect it had on your life. What changes have you implemented in order to be a good *Compass Father* to each of your children? What changes are you still seeking to implement?

THE COMPANION FATHER

I am with you and will watch over you wherever you go...I will

not leave you until I have done what I have promised you.

- Genesis 28:15 <small>NIV</small>

Determining to Be a Dad
Who's Always There

ood, I'm glad you're sitting by me. Sometimes I throw up." Not exactly the kind of welcome you want to hear from the airline passenger occupying the seat next to yours. Then, before the gentleman could stow his bag into the overhead locker, his youthful "seat mate" managed to share his name, age and itinerary: "I'm Billy Jack. I'm fourteen, and I'm going home to see my daddy."

Young Billy Jack was flying solo, literally, the day he sat next to well-known author and preacher Max Lucado on an airplane headed to the boy 's home and his dad. Lucado wrote of the encounter, telling how this friendly, loving little boy in a big body admitted needing someone to look after him because he got confused a lot. Whether the flight attendants served food or the drink cart arrived or any attendant simply passed by, Billy Jack would remind them that he was traveling alone and needed all the help he could get, always ending with "Don't forget to look after me."[1]

There's a little bit of Billy Jack in most of us, and none more so than children, for life is a journey no child should be called on to travel alone. They are vulnerable travelers who need a father figure to accompany and help them along the way. What the Creator said of His first human offspring could be equally said of all children: "It's not good for the Man to be alone; I'll make him a help, a *companion.*"[2]

The apostle Paul, one of the early church fathers, clearly understood man's need for companionship and a father's role towards his children. When recalling his time spent connecting with a group of Christians in the city of Thessalonica, he remarked, "With each of you we were like a father with his child, holding your hand, whispering encouragement, showing you step-by-step how to live well before God, who called us into his kingdom, into this delightful life."[3] To Paul, fatherhood involved companionship.

My own father tried hard to be a companion-type of dad. He was always there for me and my brother but, like many dads, he struggled with the issue of time. Working incredibly long hours to establish a successful hardware business in the industrial heart of the United Kingdom was his way of expressing his love for his children. Still, occasionally he found a little time to enjoy his hobbies of fishing, carpentry and stamp collecting.

On the few occasions he took off from work to be with his sons he loved nothing better than to spend the day fishing. Memories of father/son fishing expeditions with the early morning mist rising off the lake and the sound of birds singing remind me of how precious and effective those times of companionship were. Bonding with a busy father is never easy, but my life was made the better for his willingness to companion me in the best way he knew how.

In stark contrast to my own experience, Barack Obama, 44th U.S. President, knew little of the companionship of a loving father. Speaking out about his absent dad, he said, "At the time of his death, my father remained a myth to me, both more and less than a man. He had left…when I was only two years old, so that as a child I knew him only through the stories that my mother and grandparents told."[4]

Countless children everywhere travel fatherless through life. Their heart's cry is the same as Billy Jack's declaration to the flight attendants: "Don't forget to look after me." Kids like these are left stranded on the shores of loneliness. Absentee dads (whether physically or emotionally) cause their children to miss out on the love, learning, laughter, leadership and lasting care of a protective male. Society is notorious for fostering this style of fatherhood. In so doing we have created a fatherless generation that is suffering from a *hate* it cannot handle, and a *hurt* it cannot heal because it is continuously flying solo through life.

"Kids who grow up in families without a father or where the father is distant and uninvolved are more likely to drop out of school, start smoking, abuse drugs, become teen parents, have psychological and social problems, turn to violence, and end up in jail," says parenting books author Armin Brott. "Being there from the start is no guarantee that your kids will never suffer any of these problems, but there's no question that your children will be happier, healthier, and more successful with you than without you."[5]

Young people who lack the loving, caring presence of a dad often voice their need for companionship by acting out destructive behavior. So this chapter is going to tackle that problem by shedding light on what it truly means for fathers to be their children's best friend through the next essential characteristic of a dad — the *Companion Father*.

Table Time

Fathering involves developing a close connection with our children, which is one definition of *companion*. Another dictionary describes a *companion* as "a traveler who accompanies you" or "a comrade in arms." Interestingly, the Latin root from which we get our English translation of *companion* has the idea of "eating a meal with someone" or "sharing bread together" (*com* = "with" or "together" and *panis* = "bread").[6] Add to this the biblical symbolism of *bread* being a life sacrificially surrendered so that others might live life to the full,[7] and the picture we get of the *Companion Father* is this: a person willing to sacrificially share the very basics of human life with someone they love, so that they can live, laugh, love, learn and create a lasting legacy *together*.

Consider the implications of these definitions. For instance, it's possible that a father/child relationship could, for all intents and purposes, be called *table time*. Perhaps, then, the most vital piece of household furniture for a family would be the dining table, as in one sense it is the "altar" around which the lives of our children are shaped and shielded from outside influences. Mealtimes give us an opportunity to enjoy eating with our family without any media distraction or family members disappearing into separate rooms.

When dads uphold the family mealtime, they demonstrate a level of love and commitment that provides assurance and comfort to all the family. By sharing food and conversation, we enter into and enjoy "the bread of life," making the table more "an altar than an eating counter."[8] In a way, these dads practice a priestly responsibility. It's at the meal table that social, spiritual and mental renewal can take place during a moment of time, regularly spent, in which fathers can help their children's spirits be reborn, their minds refreshed and their bodies revived.

Being at major mealtimes whenever possible is just one of the simple ways we can companion our kids. Many fathers choose to forget or forgo this and other companionship opportunities for the sake of time and personal convenience. They don't realize that they are passing up some of the richest memories of fatherhood, along with a great opportunity to impact their kids.

The DNA of Dads

Although it's uncertain how many children King Solomon actually had, to ask God for wisdom is a shrewd move for a man with seven hundred wives! Known by many as the wisest man who ever lived and having written the bulk of the Old Testament Proverbs, there's perhaps no better place to find wise parental advice than from his writings, for "the Proverbs are meant to be to our practical life what the Psalms are to our devotional life."[9]

An anthology of practical thoughts and wisdom from a father to his son (fifteen times the writer uses the phrase "my son"), Solomon wrote the book of Proverbs to give his children a guidebook for successful living. Using the Hebrew word *ra'ah* translated "close friend," "companion," "neighbor" or "buddy,"[10] he presented us with a collection of scriptures that create five parental pillars on which to build a sound biblical image of fatherhood. Here, then, is the *Companion Father's* DNA, for this kind of dad is someone who…

Loves unconditionally —

Proverbs 17:17 says it this way, "A friend ["companion"[11]] loves at all times." In other words, a *Companion Father* loves at all times regardless of the circumstances. Although we may have preferred it if parenting came with a "prenuptial" agreement, it didn't. There's no precursor to childcare, no 'get out' clause to stop loving and caring for those life has placed in our charge. All our children deserve a love without reserve no matter what they say or do and an understanding that no matter how inconvenient, we're always there for them.

Just as our heavenly Father shows us unconditional love in that as a Christ follower there is nothing I can say or do that will make God love me any more or any less, His is the perfect example of both affection and availability. Our Father/God "will neither slumber nor sleep"[12] and is accessible for His children 24/7.

The kind of parental love Solomon refers to in Proverbs 17:17 is the love a father has for his son. It's a *sacrificial love* whereby Abraham laid everything on the line for the sake of his son Isaac's long-term legacy.[13] It's the love Jacob had for his son Joseph, a *demonstrative love* that caused him to become a doting dad who gave his favorite son an expensive multi-colored jacket.[14]

Although somewhat unwise, Jacob's action highlighted the fact that men tend to respond with a love that leaps into action, rather than a love that pays attention. That doesn't always carry over to our children nowadays.

"All too frequently, parenting — especially fathering — receives the leftovers," says Dr. Kevin Leman, internationally known psychologist and author. "After work, after golf, after the car gets fixed and the football game is over, then, if nothing else needs to be done, the father will make time for his children."[15]

While such behavior might be the preferred material of your average TV sitcom or the subject of a favorite daddy joke, the reality is no laughing matter, for a love that listens is a "love [that] cares more for others than for self."[16] This kind of love is a two-way street. Leftover fathers "are missing out on the most fulfilling and most influential work they could ever do."[17]

Lives genuinely —

Proverbs 19:4 says it this way: "Wealth attracts friends as honey draws flies, but poor people are avoided like a plague"(MSG). In another Proverb, Solomon described having wisdom as being wealthy.[18] For the *Companion Father*, wealth in verse 4 could be translated as teaching his children the true value of life.

A father named Reginald James Poitier taught his son, Sydney, that the true value of a human life is not in the color of a person's skin but in the depth of their character. Reflecting on his own journey, Sidney credits his dad's *companionship* for "equipping him with the unflinching sense of right and wrong and of self-worth that he has never surrendered and that have dramatically shaped his world."[19] That wealth of wisdom carried over into Sydney's career as an award-winning actor; he "wasn't going to play any part that might dishonor his values."[20]

The distorted perception of fatherhood portrayed by the media undermines a child's image of a dad which ultimately undervalues the true meaning of life. Robert Coles wrote on this subject in a five-volume series, *Children of Crisis,* which ran to more than a million words, earning him a Pulitzer Prize in 1973. Having spent twenty-five years travelling the world, cataloguing the effects of poverty and wealth on children, he discovered that the poor are mysteriously blessed and that the rich live in peril. He learned in the process that, "what matters most comes not from without — the circumstances of life — but from within, inside the heart of an individual boy or girl."[21] What he also found was, "Nothing I discovered about the make-up of human beings contradicts in any way what I learn from the Hebrew prophets, and from Jesus and the lives of those he touched."[22]

The *Companion Father* teaches his children the true values of life by modeling his heavenly Father in whom there is "nothing two-faced, nothing fickle."[23] For fathers to *live genuinely*, then, not only requires that they talk biblical principles but also that they realistically live the Christ-like life in front of their children in such a way that attracts to, rather than distracts from, the Christian faith.

Gives generously —

Proverbs 19:6 says it this way: "Many seek the favor of a generous man, and everyone is a friend to a man who gives gifts." True friendship is never an issue of finance, and fatherhood is never a matter of becoming some kind of Al Bundy cash cow — the image of Bundy's role as a father in the American sitcom *Married with Children.* In that show he is seen as nothing more than the sole source of obligatory handouts.

The hallmark of true parental companionship is a generous spirit, but not in the Al Bundy sense. A willingness to spend time and connect with our children, even if that means cashing in on personal preferences, reflects the generous nature of a man, as Solomon talked about.

The constant readiness to give oneself away for the sake of cultivating and maintaining a strong connection with our children is the foundational pillar on which we build a strong father/child relationship. Given the choice, every one of our kids would rather enjoy our *presence* than our *presents*. To give ourselves away in terms of time, energy, resources and schedule in those memorable moments of connecting with our children is priceless.

Maybe what sparked Solomon's comments concerning the true

nature of companionship were stories he heard about his father, King David's close friend Ahithophel and how they both enjoyed "long hours of leisure"[24] together. Whatever it was, Solomon saw companionship as having its own unique attraction, for which all humans long. Using the appealing nature of a generous, giving man, Solomon described the caliber of a close friend as someone who intentionally gives of himself to others—the trade mark of the *Companion Father*.

Working to create the wherewithal to provide for his children's welfare and general well-being, this type of dad does whatever it takes to be there and facilitate the ongoing development of his family. Maybe a father escorts his daughter on a date night, so as to show her how a gentleman should treat a lady. Or a dad walks through with his son how a guy behaves towards a member of the opposite sex by demonstrating love and respect for the boy's mother. The bottom line is, "Through his companionship, attitudes, and warm approval, a father has the opportunity to instill and call forth deep qualities and strengths in his [son and] daughter."[25]

Memorable moments we create with our kids remain with them throughout their lives and help to build confidence in who they are and what they can do. It's the biblical hallmark of a *Companion Father:* he knows how to give "good gifts to [his] children," and he gives his all.[26] That kind of giving reflects what well-known author and pastor Gary Chapman describes as a child's "love language." Be it quality time (doing everyday life *together*); words of affirmation; gifts; acts of service or physical touch;[27] a father should *give generously* gifts that will promote spiritual, physical, emotional and social growth in his children.

Speaks encouragingly —

Proverbs 22:11 says it this way: "He who loves purity of heart, and whose speech is gracious, will have the king as his friend." The words of King David's close companion[28] and confidante, Ahithophel, were so legendary[29] that they inspired the lyrics of a song.[30] Perhaps it was this example that motivated Solomon to write about another key facet of friendship that is related to fatherhood: grace-filled speech. There's no more supportive pillar of fatherhood that builds strong children than encouraging words.

Solomon describes this kind of speaking in other verses of Proverbs. In one he says, "Faithful are the wounds of a friend";[31] meaning that a father's words may need to be painful at times (like telling a child no for his or her own good). But Solomon also writes that our words should always be like "oil and perfume" that "make the heart glad," because the true fragrance or "sweetness of a friend comes from his earnest counsel."[32]

However, the key to using effective words is timing. The right words might be a blessing, but spoken at the wrong time they become a curse. Hence Solomon's advice that reads, "If you wake your friend in the early morning by shouting, 'Rise and shine!' it will sound to him more like a curse than a blessing."[33]

I may be a public speaker and a published author, but the right words at the wrong time have been my Achilles heel in terms of fatherhood. Trying to wake my sleepy kids from their spiritual, moral, financial and social slumber might appear admirable, but what was initially intended as a blessing has all too often become the "Curse of the Daddy." While often operating on the philosophy "If it needs to be said, it needs to be said now," my children would have been served better if I'd heeded the proverb, "Congenial conversation—what a pleasure! The right word at the right time—beautiful."[34] If life ever got ugly in my relationship with my children, and for that matter with my wife, it was more often than not because I failed to engage brain before opening mouth.

To physically be there for our children as they journey through life is commendable, but to sit in silence is inexcusable. "If you limit yourself to cursory conversations stolen during station breaks, all you will have to show for your time and effort later in life is a distant, detached relationship with your son or daughter."[35] Or as Solomon so aptly put it in another verse in Proverbs: "Words satisfy the mind as fruit does the stomach; good talk is as gratifying as a good harvest. Words kill, words give life; they're either poison or fruit—you choose."[36] A good father speaks *gracious* or encouraging words along the way. Regardless of what a child says or does, the *Companion Father's* ongoing conversations open up new vistas of opportunity, rather than valleys of despondency.

In a society where some parents feel free to publicly shout and swear at their kids, it appears that tomorrow's social problems are being seeded through foul-mouthed parents who have forgotten the biblical truth that, "Death and life are in the power of the tongue."[37] In direct opposition to this kind of venomous talk, the *Companion Father* uses every possible opportunity to *speak encouragingly* and communicate kindness and potential to his children.

I like how Mo Vaughn, a Major League first baseman, once described this: "Yelling doesn't communicate. It's a whisper in somebody's ear. It's a pat on the back. It's a push, at times. Whatever you need to do to communicate. It's not jamming someone up against the wall. It's learning what you can and cannot say to each individual to get the best out of them."[38]

Sticks closely –

Proverbs 18:24 says it this way: "Friends come and friends go, but a true friend sticks by you like family" (MSG). Solomon saw true companionship as having an adhesive quality to it, reminding us that the *Companion Father* sticks to his children with a loving permanence of parental superglue.

When the Old Testament character Ruth refused to leave her mother-in-law Naomi, she said while "clinging" to her, "Where you go I will go."[39] In this incident we see something of the "stickablity" Solomon had in mind. For the phrase "a true friend *sticks* by you" has the thought of two people experiencing a "lasting attachment," as in the functional "joining together" of two halves of a hinge.

Describing the friendship of David and Jonathan the Scriptures tell us, "The soul of Jonathan was knit [welded] to the soul of

David."[40] It's this degree of closeness that is a key ingredient of the Hebrew word *ra'ah* translated "friend" or "companion" that Solomon uses throughout Proverbs as he endeavors to give a picture of companionship that's like:

- Clinging to someone you love — Genesis 2:24
- Being deeply attached to an individual — Ruth 1:14; Genesis 34:3
- Holding on no matter what — 2 Samuel 20:2
- Linking of two pieces of armor — 1 Kings 22:34; 2 Chronicles 18:33
- Scales on a snake or fish — Job 41:23

Add to this the thought of joining or fastening two pieces of cloth, a shepherd staying in close relationship to his sheep, the joining of two human bones in order to function correctly, and you begin to get the idea of the true essence of biblical companionship *and* fatherhood.

Being "near [in spirit],"[41] or just having our children in our thoughts is too ethereal for Solomon's liking. True companionship seen throughout Proverbs involves "availability" and "closeness," a "neighborliness" that means you are available if needed; the friendship of a "school buddy," the listening ear of a "confidante," the reliability of a "special friend," and the honor of being to our children what a "best man"[42] is to a bridegroom. This is the heart of a dad who *sticks closely* to his children.

Taking fatherhood beyond mere acquaintance,[43] the five parental pillars in the book of Proverbs speak of someone who is always trying to tune in and get "on the same wave length" as his children, someone they feel free to share their innermost thoughts with,[44] a special friend who always shows them kindness, someone you know would not leave you in a crisis,[45] an advisor whose words have a calming effect,[46] someone who is always great to have around,[47] and someone you go to in time of need[48]—all of which are the true essence of being a father.

The heartache of writing this book is the fact that I am presently living thousands of miles away from my children and grandchildren. Unable to enjoy a game of golf with my boys, go shopping, spend time and have coffee with my girls, and be available to journey with my grandchildren in their formative years is for me the challenge of not being able to truly companion them. To enjoy a birthday party, Christmas lunch or family get-togethers are for me close encounters of the first kind that are essential to being a *Companion Father*. Whether dads love from a distance or are physically present, we must live intentionally to bridge the gaps of circumstances in order to walk in this dynamic.

Making a World of Difference

Children are some of the world's greatest mimics; they seem instinctively to copy the positive and negative nature of the person they're with the most. The more time our kids spend connecting with us and enjoying our company, the more likely they will model our beliefs and behavior.

Talking with our kids regularly is important, but knowing what to say to them is not always necessary. Just the presence of a caring, loving dad can make a world of difference to his children as evidenced by a powerful story that's told of a teenage boy who lived alone with his father. The two of them enjoyed a very special relationship, especially in the son's love of sports. Accompanying his son to every football match he was involved in, the father never missed an opportunity to cheer his son from the stands, even though the boy spent the whole time warming the substitute's bench.

Although the boy was the smallest in his high school class, his father continued to encourage him to pursue his passion while making it clear he didn't have to play football if he didn't want to. But the lad loved the game and was determined to hang in there. Giving of his very best at every practice, he wondered if maybe he'd get to play when he became a senior.

All through high school he never missed a practice. All four years his dad was his number one fan and faithful companion who attended every match so as to cheer him on from the stands and shout words of encouragement to a boy who never left the bench.

When the young man went to college, he decided to try out for the football team as a "walk-on." Everyone was sure he could never make the cut, but he did. The coach admitted that he kept him on the roster because he always put maximum effort for minimum rewards into every practice and, at the same time, provided the other members with the spirit and hustle they badly needed.

Excited with the news that he had survived the cut, he rushed to the nearest phone and called his dad to share in the excitement and to expect season tickets for all the college games.

This persistent young athlete never missed practice during his four years at college, but he also never got to play in the game. It was the end of his senior football season, and as he trotted onto the practice field shortly before the big play-off game the coach met him with a telegram. Upon reading the message he became deathly silent. Swallowing hard, he mumbled to the coach, "My father died this morning. Is it all right if I miss practice today?" The coach put his arm gently around his shoulder and said, "Take the rest of the week off, son. And don't even plan to come back to the game on Saturday."

Saturday arrived, and the game was not going well. In the third quarter, when the team was ten points behind, a silent young man quietly slipped into the empty locker room and put on his football gear and ran onto the sidelines. The coach and players were astounded to see their faithful teammate back so soon.

"Coach, please let me play. I've just got to play today," pleaded the young man. The coach pretended not to hear him. There was no way he wanted his worst player in this close play-off game. But the young man persisted and finally, feeling sorry for the kid, the coach gave in.

"All right," he said, "you can go in." Before long, the coach, the players and everyone in the stands could not believe their eyes. This little unknown who had never played before was doing everything right.

The opposing team could not stop him. He ran, he passed, blocked and tackled like a star. His team began to triumph. The score was soon tied. In the closing seconds of the game, this kid intercepted a pass and ran all the way for the winning touchdown! The fans broke loose. His teammates hoisted him onto their shoulders amidst the cheering crowd.

Finally, after the stands had emptied and the team had showered and left the locker room, the coach noticed that the young man was sitting quietly in the corner all alone. The coach came to him and said, "Kid, I can't believe it. You were fantastic! Tell me what got into you? How did you do it?"

Looking up at the coach and with tears in his eyes, he said, "Well, you knew my dad died, but did you know that my dad was blind?"

The young man swallowed hard and forced a smile, "Dad came to all my games, but today was the first time he could see me play, and I wanted to show him I could do it!"[49]

Personal Reflections / *Checklist for Companions:*

Of the five characteristics listed in this chapter that describe the characteristics of the *Companion Father*, grade yourself on a scale of 1—10 (*ten being so good you could not possibly improve*). Also, list ways in which you might improve at least **three** of the five characteristics.

• **Loving Unconditionally**—[1 2 3 4 5 6 7 8 9 10—Circle one]
How I intend to improve: _____

• **Living Genuinely**—[1 2 3 4 5 6 7 8 9 10—Circle one]
How I intend to improve: _____

• **Giving Generously**—[1 2 3 4 5 6 7 8 9 10—Circle one]
How I intend to improve: _____

• **Speaking Encouragingly**—[1 2 3 4 5 6 7 8 9 10—Circle one]
How I intend to improve: _____

• **Sticking Closely**—[1 2 3 4 5 6 7 8 9 10—Circle one]
How I intend to improve: _____

Group Discussion

Share the grades you gave yourself on all five characteristics and how you intend to improve on three of them. Ask for some general observations on how practical your proposed areas of improvement are and ask someone within the group with whom you feel comfortable to be accountable to ask you the hard questions next time you meet. For instance, "How am I doing in improving those three aspects of fatherhood shared last time with the group?" and "What have been the wins in this exercise in my role as father?"

THE COMPOSER FATHER

DEDICATION

1971–1981

To Julie Bennett who for a few short years,

with the help of her heavenly father,

sang her beautiful song & turned

her disability into God's ability

so as to brighten the lives of all

who journeyed with her.

Determining to Be a Dad
Who Facilitates the Song

The birth of a child is meant to be a time of celebration, but for Patrick John Hughes the eerie silence of the delivery suite made it abundantly clear that this was not a rejoicing moment. Up to this point the pregnancy and birth of his son, Patrick Henry, had been uneventful and the baby, at first glance, seemed to have all the necessary bits and pieces. Then Patrick John overheard someone in the room use the phrase "multiple anomalies."

The facts surrounding Patrick Henry's birth were devastating. Born with no eyes and a tightening of the joints that restricted the use of his arms and legs, Patrick's parents faced a crisis of faith that would require both the grace of God and the gift of music to see them through the dark days ahead.

When the doctors explained the extent of his son's disability, that was the moment when "the dream died" for this father. Having mentally mapped a spot in the backyard to play ball with his boy, Patrick John's field of dreams had been turned into a pit of despair. Battling thoughts of multiple surgeries, pain and suffering for a son who would never be able to walk or stand on his own, let alone pitch or catch a ball, the future looked grim. Yet, with typical male bravado, Patrick John wanted to push through the problem, fix it and move on. All he could do, though, was face the reality that his son was severely disabled and would desperately need the tender love and care of his parents for the rest of his life.

Several months later Patrick John was looking forward to babysitting his young son one evening as it would be an ideal opportunity for some father/son bonding, especially when he believed that putting young Patrick Henry to bed would be no big deal. The normal bedtime routine, however, was ruined by a baby who had decided to exercise his lungs with a bout of incessant crying. Having tried everything to pacify the baby, Patrick John was running out of ideas when, suddenly, he spotted the piano in the corner of the room.

"He stood up, walked over to the piano, and laid my blanket on the top, "a grown up Patrick Henry later described in his book, *I Am Potential*. "Our piano is a high upright … laying me on my back on the blanket … He moved me closer to the wall, and I seemed stable, but I was still screaming bloody murder. Now what? My dad is a musician…so he sat quickly and started softly playing a lullaby. *Boom!* I stopped crying immediately. Dad was amazed. I was so quiet he checked to make sure I was still breathing. I was. He said a quick thank you prayer and started playing again, this time something more upbeat. It was a miracle!

The angels in heaven were probably looking down at him and laughing out loud, saying, 'I knew that thick-headed young man would figure it out sooner or later'."[1]

By the time he was nine months old, Patrick Henry was already sitting up in his highchair at the piano, pounding the keys as heaven began to sweeten the bitter disappointment of physical disability with the gift of music and song. Soon able to play a number of simple tunes, his exceptional musical talent meant that "at the age of two, he was taking requests. By grade school he was playing old standards and by high school he was playing the blues"; by the time he was in college he had become "an accomplished pianist and trumpet player."[2]

In recent times this father/son team became members of the Louisville University Marching Band. How does a blind trumpet player who relies on a wheelchair for mobility compete in a marching band? With the help of a dedicated dad who not only attends his son's classes, but learns the various marching routines in order to push his son's wheelchair during the band's half-time performance. All this is possible because his dad works the graveyard shift at UPS.

It's been said that life is not about waiting for every storm to pass but about learning to sing in the rain.[3] Patrick John helped his son resonate with the divine purpose God had for his life. A dad who is willing to do whatever it takes to empower his children to become the song God intended, even when it means "singing in the rain," personifies what may be the most out-of-the-box aspect of fatherhood covered here yet — the *Composer Father*.

This attribute of fatherhood revolves around a dad ensuring that his children sing their own unique inner song. It is best accomplished when fathers have a working knowledge of the biblical score from which all music must ultimately flow.

Music — the Language of God

Leonard Bernstein, world-renown composer and conductor, "was fond of pontificating from his conductor's perch that the best translation of the Hebrew in Genesis 1 was not 'and God said' but 'and God *sang*'."[4] It's even rumored that the celebrated composer once compared creation to a musical composition that constantly sings back its praise to God. However, Bernstein is not the only one advocating that creation is basically a musical composition. Famed author C. S. Lewis may have alluded to this in Book 6 of his *Chronicles of Narnia — The Magician's Nephew*. Lewis seems to suggest that when Aslan the lion created Narnia he did so by singing everything into existence — as he sang things began to appear from the ground.[5]

Even science suggests that all matter is simply "vibrating threads of energy" and that "sound is the energy formed by vibrations," so that you "put sound and rhythm together and you get…music."[6] Science unintentionally has aligned itself with the biblical idea that when God created man and matter He simply composed a song that was intended to sing His praises throughout the eternal ages. The fall of man in the Garden of Eden, however, made all things discordant with the original score. Since then, God has always been looking for sons and daughters who will join together in an anthem of exaltation until the whole of creation resonates with praises to the one and only true God.

The New Testament speaks of a coming cosmic crescendo, a moment in time when God will wrap up this present age and His entire creation will once again become an orchestral accompaniment heard throughout the universe, as heaven and earth harmonize together. It's towards this grand finale that the Holy Spirit works endlessly to tune the hearts of men and women so they might learn the lyrics of heaven and begin to practice eternal praise.

All humanity (past, present and future) is invited to this forthcoming cosmic event, yet not all will participate, for this is the song of the redeemed, a melody made only for those whose lives are in tune with the purpose of God. Discordant (rebellious) humanity desperately needs the retuning work of the Holy Spirit that comes through a personal faith in Jesus Christ and receiving Him as Savior and Lord. As the tuning fork of heaven, Jesus alone is the One who can recalibrate our inharmonious lives to the extent that our broken chords "will vibrate once more" [7] and our hearts will be tuned to sing His grace. So once again we see that it is God who exemplifies the ultimate character trait of fatherhood that we're looking at — in this case the *Composer Father*.

This idea that there is potentially a musical element in all matter may be why Pythagoras, the ancient Greek philosopher and inventor of geometry, concluded that "a stone is frozen music" [8] or why scripture reminds us that if humanity fails to sing God's praise, then creation itself will fill the void as "the [very] stones will cry out."[9] Isn't this what the hymn writer meant when these words were penned?

"This is my Father's world,

and to my listening ears

all nature sings, and round me rings

the music of the sphere."[10]

How true those statements are when we understand that "every time a bud bursts and a flower appears, a sound is made. …Everything that is has sound and rhythm—from otters and octopi to quails and quasars. Fin whales can easily hear the bleeps of other fin whales 4,000 miles away; some scientists argue 13,000 miles away, humpbacks often sing in rhyme, and the songs they sing are always changing while at the same time they are passed from male to male."[11]

Music and song have always been an integral part of God's creation, for when God "laid the foundation of the earth …the morning stars sang together and all the sons of God shouted for joy."[12] Yet, since the discordant work of the fall, "creation waits with eager longing"[13] for that orchestral crescendo yet to sound when, in "the fullness of time," God will "unite all things in [Christ], things in heaven and things on earth."[14] The greatest celestial crescendo is yet to come!

Good Vibes

When God created man, he composed a song, the reality of which may be still evident in the way we describe interpersonal relationships. We talk about being in or out of tune with each other, being on the same wave length with a person, as well as giving off good or bad vibes. (Maybe the Beach Boys got it right when they sang their famous song "Good Vibrations"!)

That all humans are a song is seen in the fact that we're all born with a measure of musical ability. Although not necessarily the next Beethoven or John Lennon, all babies have the capacity to create and appreciate music. In each of us there is an inner song waiting for the right environment to burst forth in praise to our Creator. God created in all of us a unique, one-of-a-kind, unrepeatable, irreplaceable song, an original musical composition, a divine investment that needs an opportunity to be heard. Childhood is where it all begins, for children, unlike many adults, have the inherent ability to sing their song without a moment's hesitation or inhibition.[15]

Believing we're all born with a song, psychotherapist and play therapist Roger Day reminds us, "For nine months [a child] has listened to the rhythms of heart, lung and digestive system of [their] mother. He has learned to recognize the cadence and tempo of his mother's — and father's — voice. By the time he is born he is bursting with music, rhythm and movement."[16] All the more reason that the early months of childhood should be filled with music and song.

Parents who play intuitively with their children move their hands rhythmically, singing and cooing to their babies. Conversely, deprived children lack not only the social interaction of loving parents but also the musical stimulation necessary to appreciate the rhythm of their inner song. Deprived children usually become stunted, stifled and ultimately totally silenced. Roger Day was one of the few deprived kids who didn't.

Empathizing with the movie character August Rush from the film of the same name, Roger grew up in a musical family who made him feel inadequate and musically inept but, like August , at the age of eleven Roger says, "I began to walk the woods and hills alone, away from home. Intuitively, I skipped and danced through the leaves, listening to the wind and birds as I sang to the sky. However, unlike August, my song didn't bring me closer to my parents but to God, my heavenly Father, who had created men. In nature, with no musical training, I found my song."[17]

Our song will not always be heard in the musical tones of chorus and verse. For some, the melody of their song will be heard in the continual humming of an unknown tune or the rhythm of a beat to which they skip, dance or play. For others, it means finding a way to harmonize with that silent symphony which they alone are aware of—a piece of artwork, a sudden smile, an infectious laugh—for, ultimately, everything can bring praise to God when it harmonizes with the music of heaven.

"Everyone has an inner song," wrote Vanessa Nowitzky, a singer for Rogue Opera's school tour program, "yet almost no one is aware of it…. The inner song I have named is a constant, ongoing music within each being. Young children voice their inner song through their whole bodies just as they hear it, until they are trained or constrained not to. I am sure…you have observed that children, especially under the age of eight, tend to hum their way through their days."[18] Composing fathers can facilitate their children's songs — be it the unintelligible sounds of a baby or the joyful shouts of a young child — when these dads take the time and make the effort that's necessary.

Orphaned fledgling songbirds are creatures in crisis. Needing food, shelter, affection and a mate, they must learn how to voice their song. In the same way a child is taught a language, young male songbirds learn to sing from their fathers. Each song they learn carries a vital piece of information about such things as sex and lineage. Passed down from generation to generation, these songs are crucial to the ongoing survival of the species.

In caring for orphaned birds, some care-workers in the United Kingdom have had to go to extraordinary lengths to rectify the problem of absent parents. Realizing that "female birds in many species choose a partner based on the way they sing and birds learn to sing from their parents," and that "being reared in captivity can mean they don't know how to sing properly,"[19] these care-workers have created an environment in which orphaned birds listen to the pre-recorded songs of adult birds. In so doing, orphans learn to sing their song, find a mate, avoid danger and become everything life intended them to be.

Perhaps that's why "the Shavante tribe in South America begin boys on their initiation into adulthood [by having] the elders of the tribe stand the boys in a line and compel them to learn the songs"[20] they believe are vital to adult life. Or it may be why some African tribes have a singing ritual whereby "parents who are preparing for the birth of their child sit under a tree until a melody is heard which celebrates the coming of the child.

While the infant is still in the womb, and throughout the child's life, the parents sing to their children this special song for him/her." It could be why in some Native American cultures "when a child…becomes mean-spirited, ill-tempered or broken-hearted — the child is sent outside to sit on the ground and hum" until it regains what he or she has lost.[21]

Whatever the purpose in these various activities, it's clear that the involvement of the parent is paramount and that fathers in particular, have a responsibility to enable their children to say or sing, in the words of the blind hymn writer Fanny Crosby, "This is my story, this is my song."

The Composition of a Composer
The *Composer Father*, then, is someone who figures strongly in the role of enabling a child to sing their inner song. That is his major responsibility as a dad. A godly father, he leads his family the same way a conductor directs an orchestra or a choirmaster leads the choir. Appreciating each child's talent and unique contribution, he gives them all an opportunity to play their part and be heard. Releasing rather than restricting, the *Composer Father* lovingly leads his children in a way that brings the best sound out of them. What does it take to be a composer?

It seems to me that most people involved in musical composition agree that there are six key elements — and each of these has a direct bearing on being a dad. To get a greater understanding of the *Composer Father* we're going to look at each one individually.

1. *Originality*.

First and foremost, fatherhood, like composing, involves *originality*. For it's not *our* song we want our children to sing, but their own unique, one-of-a-kind, irreplaceable symphony of praise which they alone can bring. As fathers we are in constant danger of reproducing copies, plagiarizing praise, for the sake of cultural norms. Fearful our children will not fit the mold and become appreciated, approved or accepted by others, we tend to manipulate their lives to mimic what we perceive is socially acceptable. In our doing so, many children miss out on what my old university professor called, "The Individuality of Otherness."

A composer accepts that there are certain unchangeable rules and values in the construction of music and song, and he or she works on the premise that within those restrictions there are endless possibilities. It's this variation on a theme that the *Composer Father* understands. Without messing with biblical values and God's ordained order, the *Composer Father* not only encourages, he does his best to facilitate originality, remembering that God wove our children in their mother's womb with diversity, not uniformity, in mind.

Set in a mining community in Northern England where cultural norms are well entrenched, the film *Billy Elliot,* and subsequently an outstanding Broadway musical, depicts a father's struggle with his son's *originality.* Central to the plot is a young lad's aspirations to become a professional ballet dancer and a coal mining dad who struggles with his son's interest in the arts. Preferring that his boy take up the more masculine sport of boxing, Billy's dad does all he can to stifle his son's "song." However, when Mr. Elliot eventually takes time off from his own personal interests to watch his son dance, he's left with no option but to acknowledge the boy's passion and potential. True to form, this *Composer Father* took on the costly task of facilitating an audition to the Royal Ballet School, to which Billy was accepted as a student.

While we're all born originals, many of us will die copies. Leaving this world the poorer, non-originals never get the opportunity to share their unique contribution to the symphony of life. Having never been given parental encouragement to dance, sing, paint, invent, write or aspire to those things they so desperately want to do, they live their whole lives playing on the one string that circumstances have afforded them.

2. *Time.*

Copies take a few minutes to create, but originals take *time.* That's why the *Composer Father* needs to learn how to pace himself for the long-haul, realizing that fatherhood is a marathon, not a hundred yard dash. Take Bill Hewson, for instance. He not only encouraged his son to voice his own unique contribution, but understood the requirement of giving his children the *time* necessary to develop their song.

Although a frustrated musician himself, Bill loaned his son money and gave him a year's free board and lodgings to allow his struggling band the opportunity to either become a success or find a different career track. Although given the birth name Paul David, Bill Hewson's son later received the nickname Bono Vox, meaning "good voice," later shortened to Bono. He, along with the band U2, have become the outstanding singers, musicians and social activists we now know them to be — which in no small part is due to the efforts of a *Composer Father*.

At his father's funeral, Bono publicly thanked his dad who, in more ways than one, gave his son a voice. Speaking of his childhood at one point Bono revealed, "It was the kids who had to ask the father to turn [the music] down." As a *Composer Father,* Bono's dad had not only discovered his own song, but was willing to do whatever it took to help his son find his. It's said that in the lyrics of the song "Sometimes You Can't Make It on Your Own," Bono accredited his father as the person who gave him the reason to sing.[22]

3. *Mistakes.*

Composing, like fathering, takes time; there's no overnight, blockbusting success in the role of parenting — and, from starting gun to finish line, we will all undoubtedly trip up and make *mistakes*. But, like composing, *mistakes* can become a means of discovery, a much needed breakthrough. A wrong note that leads to a cool sounding chord, a switch or twist in the creative process often becomes a part of the origin and originality of a created piece of pure musical genius. As parents, we not only need to pace ourselves for the long haul and embrace our failures as learning opportunities; here's something else we need in bucketloads:

4. *Patience*.

Actor Richard Dreyfuss, playing the part of Glenn Holland in the classic Hollywood movie *Mr. Holland's Opus*, depicts the struggles and frustrations of a composer desperately trying to finish his dream of producing a grand opus. Forced to take on the position of a high school music teacher to support his family, he had little *patience* with himself or his students. Viewing his home and work life as a failure, his surprise retirement party was about to present him with a different perspective.

As a mark of appreciation for years of faithful service past and present, students gathered in the school hall to present their beloved teacher with a perfect gift—the first ever public performance of the long awaited *Mr. Holland's Opus*. Only then does this *Composer Father* realize the positive effect his life has had in helping numerous people find their own inner song.

Honoring the many unsung heroes in our schools and homes, this film not only demonstrates the need for fathers to have *patience* but the reward of doing so—if as fathers we are faithful, we will yet hear our children play their part in the symphony of praise.

5. *Inspiration*.

Just as the ancient writers needed divine *inspiration* to turn blank paper into biblical text,[23] parents need creative ability to compose the lyrics and melody that is their child's song. Fatherhood isn't hard, it's impossible. To make anything of a child's life will take all the divine help we can get. Like a sailboat driven along by the prevailing wind, [24] fatherhood needs the breeze of divine assistance. To avoid the doldrums of the uninspired drudgery some perceive parenting to be, every dad needs to experience a driving force beyond himself — a motivating breeze to impassion him and a life-giving breath to inspire him.

6. Difficulty.

Like the act of composing, fatherhood is a journey of discovery which at times is extremely *difficult.* One only has to think of the terrible twos, trying threes, frustrating fours, puberty or adolescence and no one would disagree that parenting is hard, tricky, complicated, complex, tough, demanding, tiring, strenuous, grueling, challenging…need I go on? There are moments when it seems that *God calls us into His pressure cooker and His banner over us is steam!* It's in times like this that we'd do well to remember the story of the foreign aide worker and the potter.

As a foreign visitor, the aide worker was fascinated by the way in which the medieval potter fired his clay pots. Having carefully placed the unfired vessel into the kiln, the potter would periodically withdraw the pot so as to clip the clay brim with his finger. Each time he would listen carefully to the "clunking sound" the pot made before returning it into the heat of the furnace. After repeating the exercise several times, the potter eventually heard the sound change to a "ringing tone" and his immediate response was to remove the finished pot from the fire.

Desperate to understand this strange firing process, the aide worker approached the potter. "Excuse me, sir, but why is it you keep listening to the sound of the unfired pot and only take it out of the fire when it makes a ringing sound?"

"That's simple," the potter replied. "I know when the firing is finished by the sound it makes. When the pot sings, I know it's ready to be used."

Although parenting is so difficult and at times the only sound we seem to hear is the "clunking" of children bemoaning their lot in life, be patient. "For the moment all discipline seems painful rather than pleasant, *but later* it yields the peaceful fruit of righteousness to those who have been trained by it."[25]

Fathering, like composing, requires *originality, time, mistakes, patience,* as well as a bucket load of divine *inspiration* because, although rewarding, at times being a dad is just plain *difficult!* Yet, if we will stay on the journey, we'll see the time come when the fiery process of parenting will produce the ringing tones of our children resonating with the purposes of God for their lives.

Personal Reflections

• As a father, are you someone who "sings in the rain" or are you a fair weather singer?

• As a dad, do you allow each of your children to be their own unique self?

• Is it possible that you are trying to enforce your views of what is culturally acceptable on your children through rules rather than relationship?

• In terms of your fathering experience, think of how some mistakes have been turned into learning opportunities and why.

• In considering the six characteristics of composing—*originality, time, mistakes, patience, inspiration* and *difficulty*—is there any aspect you need to improve in and, if so, how?

• Think of each of your children and consider how they are doing in terms of "singing" their inner song, such as being the person God intended them to be. How might you help them to resonate with the divine purpose for their lives?

Group Discussion

The story of Patrick Henry Hughes is a powerful message of hope and an important aspect of the role and responsibility of fatherhood. Discuss with your group what you specifically learnt from this dynamic duo and how this might alter your view of fatherhood in the future.

THE CINDERELLA FATHER

All men make mistakes,

but only the wise learn from their mistakes.

—Winston Churchill

Determining to Be a Dad
Who Turns Obstacles into Opportunities

Michael Jordan is considered to be one of the greatest basketball players of all time. Yet, it's reported that he once said, "I've missed more than 9,000 shots in my career; I've lost almost 300 games. Twenty six times I've been trusted to take the game winning shot and missed. I've failed over and over in my life. And that's why I succeed."[1] While most dads admire the expertise of their favorite sports personalities, few stop to consider just how many mistakes their heroes must have made during their sporting careers.

Actually, most household names from the world of sports, politics and entertainment have, at some point in their illustrious careers, failed to make the grade.[2] In his sophomore year, *Michael Jordan* was cut from the high school basketball team; *Albert Einstein* failed his first college entrance exam; *Charles Schulz,* the cartoonist of "Peanuts" fame, was told his cartoons were unacceptable for his high school's yearbook, and the list goes on.[3]

Wherever we stand in the spectrum of fatherhood, we all need to accept and expect the possibility that we're going to make mistakes. Whether they're small or humongous, the pathway of fathering is a steep learning curve that causes even the best of us to slip up. So, in this chapter we're going to discuss the issue of faults, fears, failure and faux pas, and look at ways to empower fathers who believe they've blown it. By using the characteristic of the *Cinderella Father* I hope to enable despondent dads to rise up from the ashes of regret and remorse and, rather than allow their mistakes to define them, choose to become fathers who sometimes fail, rather than failures who sometimes succeed.

While the faux pas of the rich and famous make tomorrow's headlines, our gaffes, no matter how huge, are not supposed to define us. Society, however, is notorious for remembering more the mistakes people have made than their successes. The truth is, if handled correctly, our misdemeanors do not have to become the signature tune by which we are remembered.

Make No Mistake, Mistakes Will Be Made

A nagging fear that plagues most men is the thought of becoming a *failure.* The possibility of being unable to perform according to other people's expectations is a ticking time bomb in the male psyche. Add to this the role and responsibility of fatherhood and the result is potentially explosive. Looking back over their feeble attempts at being a good father, many guys struggle to escape the recurring nightmare that says, "I've blown it big-time." For some, the mere sight of their children is enough to trigger a mental trip-wire that causes a belief to blow up in their face that they've screwed up the opportunity that life has afforded them to be a good dad.

Many fathers dread the thought of messing up their one and only chance at fatherhood. Convinced they don't have what it takes, they believe that somewhere, somehow they're going to make the mother of all mistakes that will leave their children emotionally scarred for life. They envision their messed up kids one day sitting on a counselor's couch sharing intimate details as to just how their father failed them.

When it comes to being a dad, you can be sure that mistakes will be made and at times failures will occur—but they don't have to be final. No matter in what age or stage of life we find ourselves, there's sufficient grace to help every failed or failing father to recover. If you feel that you have messed up or missed out, or you are desperate to rekindle a flicker of hope from the ashes of former dreams and aspirations you had for your children, keep reading. This next characteristic of fathering has one sole purpose in mind: to refuel faith and ignite hope in you.

Enacting that classic rags-to-riches children's story, the *Cinderella Father* speaks out for the down-trodden. His diction and dialogue is meant to enable despondent dads to experience a meteoric rise to new heights of fathering and become the kind of person God always intended fathers to be. So, no matter how dire your present situation, the *Cinderella Father* character is stepping into the limelight now to initiate a fairy-tale ending whereby God Himself can vindicate you if you've been wronged and validate you if you've acted righteously. It's my hope that by the time you finish this chapter, you will be inspired to believe that, by God's grace, you can go to the "celebratory ball" — in other words, you can see your dreams realized for you and your children.

The Buoyancy of Hope

I can still remember the dreams my wife and I had of building a home founded on biblical truths and raising children to become dedicated followers of Christ. Sadly, we'd presumed that the euphoria of being Christian parents was sufficient to cover the cracks that were soon to appear in our family's seemingly impregnable exterior. Rather than building a truly unsinkable "vessel," by cutting costs I had cut corners. Ignoring certain parenting essentials my bad choices in raising our kids would inevitably have severe consequences on the ongoing survival of our Christian family.

Feeling somewhat invincible, I had become indifferent to the potential danger that awaited us. Cruising through life at breakneck speed, I lacked the good sense to slow down, keep a sharp lookout, and steer a course to avoid the obstacles of which I had been warned. Like the Titanic, I didn't see the iceberg coming until it was too late. Although only a glancing blow, the damage suffered was sufficient to destroy family life as I hoped it would be.

No longer full steam ahead, we were dead in the water. "Holed" below the water line we tried to hide the truth, but the reality was the so-called unsinkable had begun to take in water. We struggled to stay afloat, as worldly influences that were supposed to be on the outside now leaked in at an alarming rate.

Christian values were being ruined by an incoming tide of post-Christian thinking. Enthusiasm to raise children in a godly way had stalled as we began to be affected by a godless culture that seemed to be deciding our destiny now. Our family was fast being overtaken by a force that my wife and I so desperately wanted to contain, but couldn't. We felt as though our family was being dragged into the abyss.

I had been a visionary father whose skills as the spiritual leader of our home had helped me to steer our family in and out of various situations, but now I felt personally responsible for the havoc I thought I had wreaked on everyone. If only I'd been more alert or maybe slowed down or taken precautions, maybe I could have saved all those "onboard." However, a growing realization that the grace of God is sufficient for any situation has enabled me to maintain my spiritual momentum and emotional equilibrium even when the circumstances of life have tried to scuttle my faith in a faithful heavenly Father.

Having hit the "icebergs" of consumerism, humanism and rationalism, the nuclear family of our society is in a crisis of Titanic proportion. In a world set on marginalizing the importance of fathers in the family, society is creating a plethora of single-parent families in which children are losing sight of the importance of a male role model. Throughout the Western world, single (and many married) dads are trying desperately to cling to the last visible remnants of their role as fathers. Christian families are no exception; the fact is the two-parent Christian family is sinking, as well.

My concern about the demise of the Christian family led me to write this book. I believe the problem is related to a dad's inability to play the part of the *Cavalier Father* who acts circumspectly; his refusal to be the *Coach* or *Cheerleader Father* who trains his children encouragingly; his unwillingness to fulfill the role of the *Compass Father* and direct his "troops" correctly; his lack of commitment as the *Companion Father* to never allow his child to fly alone; and his ignorance of the *Composer Father,* who facilitates his child's inner song intuitively.

Whatever the shortcomings of Christian dads struggling with their mistakes, they don't need finger-pointing and I told you so's. They already feel like failures and have browbeaten themselves with what I call the two "ugly sisters" of regret and remorse. (Remember the two ugly stepsisters in the *Cinderella* story?) These fathers need the buoyancy of hope, not the ballast of guilt. The good news is there's sufficient grace to bring a godly resolution to all our conflicts. We *can* function as God intended. In Him we are destined for better things as fathers!

Breaking the Cycle

Chris Gardner was destined for better things, although it didn't seem so for a while. A struggling San Francisco salesman and dad trying to make ends meet after his partner left him, Chris had no option but to care for his 5-year-old son as a single father. Having landed a great career opportunity with Dean Witter as an unpaid intern/trainee stockbroker, he had a twenty-to-one chance of being offered a permanent paid position with the firm. Without an income, the father and son duo struggled to survive as, together, they experienced the trauma of eviction, homelessness and sleeping behind the locked doors of a metro station bathroom.

As they daily sought food and shelter, Chris did his best to break out of the poverty trap and build a great future for them both. Never wanting to repeat the history of his fatherless upbringing, this *Cinderella Father* refused to abandon his child. Haunted by an abusive past and the abandonment of his own father, Chris refused to allow his son to suffer the same trauma. Chris held "one thing dearer than all else — my commitment to my son," he said, for "the most important thing that I will have ever done in my life was break the cycle of men who were not there for their children."[4]

With a fairy-tale ending, Chris Gardner refused to allow the ugliness of regret and remorse to get the better of him. Even when subjected to the inconvenience of living life among the "cinders" of homelessness, he had dogged determination to pursue his destiny, refused to be put off by the negative, and never lost hope in the dream that, one day, he and his son would "go to the ball."

The catalogue of failures listed against dads seems endless nowadays and the media berates absentee fathers who don't provide, support, visit or commit, as well as those who abuse, abandon and renege on their responsibilities. And we cannot deny the fact that some of us have made some terrible mistakes. However, like Chris, we can reach our dreams, too. The need to admit our blunders rather than apportion blame is where the healing process all begins.

In Rob Parson's excellent book *Bring Home the Prodigals,* he talks of the time when the Billy Graham organization filmed Dr. R. T. Kendall who, back then, was the senior minister at Westminster Chapel in London, England. The interview was to discuss various theological issues Dr. Kendall was addressing in his Friday evening "School of Theology." Once they had finished filming, the producer mentioned that they had a few minutes to spare and asked R.T. (as he is affectionately known) if he would talk about his family. The well-known minister immediately replied, "You don't want to know about my family. I've been a failure as a father."

Although close friends would view him as a great dad, R.T. struggled with the fact that when his children were growing up they had suffered from an absentee father who had spent too many hours doing the work of a Christian minister. However, the persistence of the producer paid off when R. T. began to talk about the various mistakes he felt he had made as a dad. None of the initial part of the interview concerning the School of Theology went public. "The only part of the film the producers ever used...was the last few minutes," shown to thousands of leaders around the world, that "said to others going through heartbreaking times — this is not just you."[5]

Get a Spiritual De-icing

Floating in amongst the flotsam and jetsam of an incoming tide of unemployment, financial hardship and broken relationships are numerous fathers who see themselves as abject failures. When listening to some of the heartrending stories these guys have to share, their self-perception is understandable.

■ My ex-wife and I split up five years ago when our two children were 5 and 7. The most difficult thing I have to deal with is not being able to see their faces everyday. *I feel I've let them down.* I haven't shared a Christmas with them in four years. I haven't seen them open their birthday present or watched their faces as they get the present they've been plaguing us for.

■ Flanked by two school friends and accompanied by his high school teacher, my drunken son stood silently on the front porch. An end-of-term school celebration had concluded with my eighteen year old now being carried to his bedroom in a drunken stupor. Unsure as to whether drugs or drink were to blame, I watched over him throughout the night and with the chime of every waking hour wondered, *Where did I go wrong?*

■ My lovely daughter has just faced a crisis of faith which has left her doubting the existence of a loving God, preferring to think that God just does as He pleases without any thought of how it might impact us human puppets. We are often left dangling high and dry at the end of the strings He controls, as and when He wills. Turning her back on church and Christianity, she is struggling to see how the sudden death of her fiancée is characteristic of a loving heavenly Father. As a pastor and father, *I feel a fraud and an abject failure* having not prepared her for a life where bad things happen to good people.

Can you empathize with any of these stories? I can, because some of them are too close to home for comfort.

In the early years of our marriage, I saw myself as potentially a perfect father, having strong opinions on how to raise happy, healthy, well-behaved, God-fearing children — then my wife became pregnant and gave birth to the first of four children! I quickly woke up to the reality that fatherhood is not that easy and, although we want to be perfect parents producing perfect children, the reality is it's always far more complicated.

At times fathers face difficult dilemmas and messy problems. Sometimes we function in a priestly manner, as the head of the home, and bring a godly resolution to those conflicts, no matter where the blame lies. Our memories of those times are sweet — but, as everyone knows, not all memories are precious. In fact, some memories are so painful that they linger and ever flood our souls.

Those kinds of memories haunt us like a bad dream from which we so desperately want to wake up. Having the ability to freeze-frame us in a moment of time, memories become the "step-mother" of past failure that confines us to the "basement" of self-doubt, guilt and despair. Incarcerated by the past, we stare endlessly into what remains of our dreams and aspirations.

Most of us have experienced the harassment of things we wished we had or hadn't done as dads: the cruel one-liners that demolished a child's dreams and aspirations; that judgmental look that mirrored our disappointment and reflected poorly on that child's sense of approval; that angry reaction instead of an affectionate response; that missed opportunity; that too-busy-to-talk, too-busy-to-listen, too-busy-to-care moment that caused us to withdraw or ignore a child looking for appreciation, approval and acknowledgment. Crystallized on the surface of our mind, bad memories act like ice on the wings of a stalled Boeing 777. Weighed down with self-loathing and emotionally stalled, we're going nowhere.

What's needed is a spiritual de-icing, what the New Testament calls "the renewal of your mind."[6] Only by putting the past in perspective, turning our mistakes into learning opportunities and bringing God-ordained closure to our mistakes can fathers be ready to soar to those heights to which we were destined. It's a process the apostle Paul describes as "forgetting what lies behind and straining forward to what lies ahead."[7]

Forgetting is not some irresponsible absent-mindedness of an overactive brain or memory lapse of an aging mind. It's an act of the will, a decision we make to not think of those things. When our heavenly Father says, "I will forgive their iniquity, and I will remember their sin no more,"[8] He isn't choosing not to visit a particular memory, not to dwell on a certain thought; but rather to think on other things or allow those thoughts to come calling.[9]

When a career move relocates us to a new address, it doesn't matter how many unwanted letters or unwelcome visitors try to interface with us at the old address; it's pointless because we've moved away *and we don't live there anymore.* Through a divine work of saving grace God is well able to "change our address" so that when the bad memories come calling, we're unable to open the door of our mind to them because we don't live there anymore. It's this principle that Paul was trying to get over to Christians when he encouraged them to, "Consider yourselves dead to sin and alive to God in Christ Jesus."[10]

Two "Ugly Sisters"

The author C. S. Lewis once described the devil's work as the business of keeping believers away from the present and the future by constantly dwelling on the past.[11] Disabled by what has already happened, we become incapacitated to live in the present and too overly occupied to be bothered with the future. At some point the two "ugly sisters" of *regret* and *remorse* step in. Let's take a look at them.

The "Ugly Sister" of Regret

Perhaps *regret* is the easier of the two to handle. It has character traits that range from disappointment to intense sorrow, feelings that can result from something you may or may not have done. In terms of fatherhood, it's a feeling linked with consequences that have resulted from people, objects or events that have negatively affected our children. For instance, a father might:

■ feel regret for a child's *bad attitude* resulting from a wrong set of beliefs he or she may have about something or someone;

■ regret a *crisis of faith* his child is going through because of something he may or may not be responsible for;

■ be struggling with his child's lack of *spiritual passion*, which he may have contributed to by either his laid-back or overly zealous approach to spiritual things;

■ regret the *choices* his children are now making as a result of those circumstances of life that he didn't adequately prepare them for or take the necessary avoiding action.

Although distant cousins, *regret* is often accompanied by *shoulda, coulda* and *woulda*. When any one of these triplets comes calling, their sole purpose in visiting is to make you feel condemned about the things you should or shouldn't have done for your children. Although most of us, given the opportunity, would love to be able to go back in time and change some things, we have to learn to deal with the consequences of our actions and break free from a life of staring wistfully into our past and whispering to ourselves, *"Shoulda, coulda, woulda."*

The "Ugly Sister" of Remorse

As ugly as *regret* is, *remorse* is far worse. While *regret* is related to a French word that means "complaint" or "lament," *remorse* comes from a Latin word that means "to bite again" and carries the thought of something that is "gnawing" away at our insides.[12] It's a feeling of guilt and self-loathing that is consuming us. Gradually destroying our sense of self-worth and general well-being, *remorse* is a more illogical type of emotion that, over time, will eat us up. Like some emotional parasite destroying us from the inside out, *remorse* can render a person incapacitated and unable to function. Draining us of hope, dreams and aspirations for either our children or ourselves, remorse will sap the lifeblood out of our ability to be the kind of father God intended us to be.

While the who-did-what-to-whom dynamic might offer us a small measure of consolation, trying to justify the unjustifiable will never silence the sisters of *regret* and *remorse.* There comes a moment in a dad's life when he has to decide that his mistakes have haunted him long enough; he has to do something about it.

Dealing with Our Past

Not that we could ever forget our failures, even if we tried—our mistakes, misdemeanors and minor discretions are mirrored in the faces and echoed in the voices of each of our children. "As if parenting wasn't hard enough anyway," writes Rob Parsons, "modern society practically forces us to see our children's lives as a judgment on whether or not we have been successful. We want our children to do well because we want to be well-thought of ourselves."[13]

When King David, in an act of contrition for his extramarital affair, cried out, "My sin is ever before me,"[14] he was clearly struggling with the consequences of his horrendous mistakes. It may have been the sight of a pregnant Bathsheba or the cries of a sick child, but something or someone served as a constant reminder of his immoral, treacherous and murderous mistakes for which he now needed to repent. Only when we're honest enough to admit our mistakes and allow the grace of God to work in us can we truly live the life of the *Cinderella Father.*

In his book *Letters to My Son,* Kent Nerburn puts it like this: "If you are haunted by personal demons that eat away at your life, if you do not have the discipline that fatherhood requires—you will live in a private shame that will drag you downward and keep you from being the father that lives in your heart. Nothing—not alcohol, not other women, not running away—will shield you from the harsh truth of your failure. So look upon fatherhood as a gift. It is one of life's common miracles, available to everyone and given freely to us all. A child, whether healthy or ill, misshapen or beautiful, opens the world into a new sunlight. It is an experience greater than a dream."[15]

Living free from things we'd rather forget involves our mentally moving away from bad memories and making ourselves unavailable to take delivery of those "thought parcels" of guilt, anger, pain and sorrow that *regret* and *remorse* try to drop off at our door. Stalled and going nowhere because of past failure, we need to experience the "de-icing" effect of God's grace to rid us of the weight of self-loathing and renew our thinking, ready for takeoff into the realm for which we were created.

In so doing, we will avoid the domino effect, whereby when something bad happens our memory bank immediately makes a deposit that takes us back to a crucial moment that the mind continually insists is the reason for all our present problems. Once again, the good is knocked over by the bad and we are left in an emotional heap on the floor.

Just as the biblical character David took five smooth stones to defeat Goliath and any of his four avenging brothers who might come after him, to live in total victory over our past we need to pick up for ourselves five proven principles from God's stream of grace. I call them the "Pebble Principle."

Recognize —

First, to deal with the personal demons of the past requires that we *recognize* both their power and presence. To act like the ostrich and bury our head in the sand is foolishness. To simply say, "Mistakes were made," in some kind of lame attempt to excuse ourselves from responsibility is not going to cut it. While some failures are real, others are imaginary creations of an overactive mind.

On numerous occasions I've left a speaking engagement thinking I'd blown it big time only to hear of people whose lives had been transformed by my so-called "failed talk." The reality is our mistakes wield an incredible power over us and those caught in the wake, and we need to respond accordingly. Breaking the cycle of regret and remorse begins by accepting that the mistake is ours. It means we own up and acknowledge it belongs to no one else — "It's mine."

Respond —

The second principle we have to pick up on is the need to *respond* positively and not react negatively to our mistakes. This is not the moment for some knee-jerk reaction, but rather a calculated response that is the result of a well thought through strategy. Not that we procrastinate and put off to tomorrow what needs to be done today, but taking sufficient time to make a godly response so that all we say and do is not fuel to the fire, but ointment to the wound. For, like pebbles in the pond, the ripple effect of our misdemeanors are often far reaching. Caught up in the wake of something we should or shouldn't have done, many of us are either thrown off course or struggle to regain our emotional equilibrium.

Repentance —

Thirdly, we need to pick up on the biblical principle of *repentance* and, if necessary, the need to make restitution to those we have offended. More than sad remorse, godly *repentance* is a change of mind leading to a change of lifestyle. It's through the act of repentance that we are able to silence the affects of the ugly sisters. Breaking the cycle of *regret* and *remorse* is rooted in godly *repentance*.

Through a work of grace, our heavenly Father enables us to change our mind about people, objects and events. By realigning our thinking, we decide to say, "Sorry," to everyone we have offended and, from now on, change the way we live. Because our mistakes have often left a path of destruction in their wake, we will need to retrace our steps and ask forgiveness of any we have upset, and involve ourselves in the work of restoring time, trust, finances, and anything else that has been lost.

Receiving —

The fourth principle is the issue of *receiving* God's grace for our past misdemeanors. If there was ever a principle we need to pick up on in order to live free, it's this one! If anyone could have struggled with his past, it would have been the apostle Paul. Yet he could say, "By the grace of God I am what I am, and his grace toward me was not in vain."[16] To daily accept the truth that *God*

is eternally committed to show unmerited, undeserved, unconditional
favor and acceptance to those who believe in Him, no matter what they
say or do, is the pebble that enables fathers to live free of their
faults, fears, failures, and faux pas.

Refusing —

Refusing is the last aspect of the Pebble Principle we need to
pick up on, and involves saying no to those daily accusations
the "ugly sisters" keep trying to deliver to our door. If allowed,
my past will polarize, penalize, demoralize and ostracize me
as a father. However, by *recognizing* the power of my mistakes,
responding rather than reacting, and *repenting* and *receiving* God's
grace, I can *refuse* to accept what regret and remorse are trying to
dump on me.

Failure Is Not an Option

Remember the earlier story of the near failed mission of the
Apollo 13? Although it seemed a failure, the team at Mission
Control refused to accept it as such. To them failure was not an
option and the situation became known officially as a "successful
failure."

While some fathers fail, others unjustifiably feel a failure. The
recognition that there is no such thing as a perfect father, let alone
perfect children, does little to rectify those wretched feelings of
if only. Yet, while the facts conspire to make us feel a failure and
silently cause us to stare endlessly into the cinders of past dreams
and aspirations we had for our children, a personal faith in God

can enable us to think differently.

As a dad I am destined for better things than metaphorically scrubbing the floors (like Cinderella did in the fairy tale) in an attempt to clean up the mess of my own poor choices and painful consequences — and so are you. I choose to refuse the involuntary incarceration forced on me by the "stepmother" of *bad memories* and "ugly sisters" of *regret* and *remorse*. I am a father who believes in the power and purpose of a sovereign God who will one day lift me from the rags of regret and robe me in the reality of the biblical truth of *household salvation.*[17]

In this, I hold to the promises of God and the prospect that one day this *Cinderella Father* will "go to the ball." I believe that I'll share in the festivities of seeing all my children enjoying a personal relationship with Jesus Christ. I encourage you to do the same.

I find comfort in the fact that the Bible is full of successful failures, principle characters in both the Old and New Testaments who blew it big time. *Adam* had a problem with his marriage, as well as his children. *Noah* preached for 120 years without a single conversion and was remembered, among other things, for his drunkenness. *Elijah* suffered from serious depression and buckled under pressure. *David* experienced moral failure. *Solomon* failed to walk in the very wisdom God had given him. *Eli* missed it as a father and a national religious leader. *Jonah* decided to disobey God. *Peter* suffered from temper tantrums that caused him to swipe off an occasional ear and swear publicly. *Yet they all had a destiny in God which they pursued, despite their tendency to make major blunders.*

"You can run the biggest drug cartel in America or win the Super Bowl," says comedian Bill Cosby. "But if you haven't claimed your children, you are not a man. No matter how useless or hopeless a father may think he is, his role is simply to be there. If he makes that commitment, he is a much better man than he thought he was."[18]

Personal Reflections

• In a world of moral, financial, spiritual and social "icebergs" that threaten to sink family life as we know it, what preventive action are you, as a parent, taking to protect your family?

• Is your family in some way "holed" below the water line and you're trying your best to hide that fact from yourself and others?

• What could the ugly sisters of *regret* and *remorse* deliver to your door that you might still sign for, and how do you intend to handle this in the future?

• In terms of your children, picture what "going to the ball" means and begin to make that the basis of your daily prayer

Group Discussion

There is a vast difference between failing and feeling a failure. Discuss how to "deal with the demons" of your past mistakes and just how you would go about picking up on the Pebble Principle.

 ## Personal Prayer

The following prayer is a tool to help us build a foundation to live free of past mistakes (it can be prayed either personally or collectively):

Heavenly Father, I'm so conscious of those areas I have failed in as a father—the things I should have done, but didn't; the things I could have done, but didn't. So I bring all my mistakes, missed opportunities, and meager attempts to be a dad and lay them at Your feet, saying, "Sorry." I ask for Your forgiveness and your help to put things right with those I have messed up and missed out with.

Now, believing that "if we confess our sins, he is faithful and just to forgive us our sins and to cleanse us from all unrighteousness" [1 John 1:9], I call on Your grace to help me turn away from those things and make up in my children where I've messed up and missed out as a father, trusting daily that Your Holy Spirit will help me to accept Your acceptance and approval of me as a dad and be able to silence the ugly sisters of regret and remorse forever. In the name of Jesus Christ, I ask these things.

Amen.

THE CLOCK FATHER

Yesterday is gone. Tomorrow has not yet come.

We have only today. Let us begin.

— Mother Teresa

Determining to Be a Dad
Who Makes the Most of Time

Well-known English journalist John Humphrys is somewhat legendary in the United Kingdom for his no-nonsense style of interviewing and always getting to the truth behind the headlines. Having spent the whole of his working life at the ringside of European history, he has had the unique opportunity to observe the social, political and economical changes over the last fifty years.

One of his first assignments for national television was to cover a film documentary on the construction of the Anglican Cathedral in Liverpool. Started some 150 years earlier, this was a venture of immense spiritual importance to the city that so impressed Humphrys that in his book, *Devil's Advocate,* he describes in detail his meeting with one particular stonemason who had worked on this magnificent project all his working life.

"I pitied the poor chap," Humphrys wrote. "There was me, dashing hither and yon, never knowing what I might be doing the next day, master of my own timetable (news editor permitting) and my own destiny. And then there was this poor chap, turning up at the same time five days a week, chipping out more stone blocks to lay on the other stone blocks he'd been chipping out the day before and the day before ad infinitum. 'Don't you get bored?' I asked him."

"Why should I?"

"Well, all you're doing is laying one stone on another year after year."

"No, I'm not," he said.

Then with one earth shattering, eye-opening, mind-blowing statement that should resonate in the heart and soul of all fathers, the stonemason replied, "I'm building a cathedral. What will you leave behind you when you die?"[1]

Proverbs 13:22 says, "A good man leaves an inheritance [of moral stability and goodness] to his children's children" (AMP). Whether we see fatherhood as monotonous, mundane or magnificent, how we spend our days shaping our children's lives so as to enable them to fit into the grand scheme of things is the most significant legacy we can leave behind. In this chapter we're going to look at what that means through the next trait of a godly dad — the Clock Father.

Something George Bernard Shaw wrote captures the essence of this idea of leaving a heritage for and through our children: "Life is no 'brief candle' to me. It's a sort of splendid torch which I've got to hold up for the moment; and I want to make it burn as brightly as possible before handing it on to future generations."[2] Teaching his children to highly value the commodity of time, the *Clock Father* is a time manager, someone who senses the importance and implications of a life well lived, a life that has the potential to leave its mark on society.

Seeds of greatness reside in all our children, latent potential that only needs an encouraging environment in which to germinate and grow. Yet while some kids seem to reach their full potential with relative ease, others struggle to make anything of their lives. In some instances it's a matter of poor experience, education or environment; in others the problem is clearly parental.

Two Roles of Fatherhood

Held back in their ongoing development, some children suffer from fathers who see their role more in terms of a *mechanical engineer* than that of an *organic gardener.*

The *engineer* type father is a more organized, calculated, analytical and fixed personality. Willing to do whatever it takes to keep the wheels of family life turning, the engineering father runs his family like a well-oiled piece of machinery. These guys find their satisfaction in making sure everything runs as smooth as clockwork. Treating children as pre-shaped cogs who merely need to be slotted into place, the engineer dad periodically appears on the scene to make a few minor adjustments, apply a few drops of encouragement on those "pieces" he perceives are working hard, and then, before excusing himself to attend a more pressing engagement, wind up the kids with unhelpful hype.

Often guilty of seeing their role as the industrious "Mr. Fix-it," engineer fathers are usually more concerned with what some call

Time Telling,[3] than the "Mr. Flexible," *organic* fathers. The organic dad is the go-with-the-flow type and has the more important task of *Clock Building.*[4] As skilled, charismatic visionaries engineer father types may have accrued great personal wealth, but in terms of building something into their children that will outlast their own lifetime, they are extremely poor.

When it comes to being a dad, I'm more your classic "oily mechanic" than your "green-fingered gardener." My Mr. Fix-it tendencies have resulted in my own fathering skills becoming more *time teller* than *clock builder.* I don't like it, but I've noticed that I can relate in some ways to the Mr. Fix-it, engineering, *time teller* father portrayed in the award-winning movie of the 1960s — *The Sound of Music.*

Raising seven children as a single parent, Captain von Trapp is a strict military disciplinarian who uses a system of whistles and commands to run his household like a well-ordered ship. Not surprising then that the organized captain finds the organic style of leadership demonstrated by the new governess somewhat challenging. The free-spirited Maria introduces the children to the delights of music, song and a more relaxed form of house rules. With a change of environment, the seeds of greatness soon begin to blossom as each child branches out into new realms of possibility.

Maria's child-rearing temperament and characteristics are a good picture of the organic gardener *Clock Father* attributes — more creative, casual, free-spirited, natural and spontaneous — but since this is a book on fathers, here's an example of a dad who exemplified organic gardener qualities. James R. Jordan prepared the ground for his now-famous son, Michael, to become what many consider to be the greatest basketball player of all time. In his book, *For the Love of the Game: My Story,* Michael wrote of his dad:

"I think my father saw some things in me that I couldn't see in myself. At first, I just thought it was a father's pride, the voice of hopes and dreams for a son to be successful.... I do believe my father knew. I believe he saw things unfolding in a way that no one, not me, not the Chicago Bulls, or anyone else, saw. I believe that's a father's gift."[5]

As a gifted organic gardener father-type, James Jordan tended to his son's ongoing development, believing that one day the seeds of greatness would germinate and grow into something phenomenal—and they did!

That the first ever father (Adam) was both groundskeeper and plantsman (established by God) perhaps is the best proof that fatherhood is better viewed through the eyes of a gardener than the goggles of an engineer. The reality, however, is that a gardener grows nothing; all he or she does is create the right environment in which those healthy plants placed in their care can grow and become everything their creator intended. The challenge is that we live in a world where creating the right environment in which children can prosper and reach their full potential is never easy.

With so many of us nowadays coming from broken homes, it's difficult to find anyone who hasn't experienced the pain of divorce or the stress of a single-parent household. Add to this mix the issue of blended families and we can see why such terms as *home*, *father* and *family* are becoming a little frayed around the edges. This, in turn, has created a confused and contradictory generation of adults who, on the one hand, might be pro-choice when it comes to abortion, yet pro-life when it comes to animals and the environment. Preferring the post-Christian mindset that has removed the riverbanks of absolute truth, the Western world (in which so many people are or soon will become parents) is awash with a go-with-the-flow type attitude that believes everything is relative and could be true.

Now more than ever the *Clock Father* is a necessary, indispensable standard by which a child's life can be ruled and regulated. Gently reminding the family that "time and tide wait for no man" and that they should all endeavor to "make the most of time," the *Clock Father* never knowingly is overbearing or too restrictive. He is a trustworthy timepiece who brings correction and control (in a godly way) to his children, and whose continued presence is comforting, not upsetting.

A Trustworthy Timepiece

In the lessons of life, it's in the handling of time that *Clock Fathers* are called to be our primary teacher. They should see and speak prophetically to their children, living prophetically towards them. In other words, fathers are to look by faith beyond the present reality of what may or may not be happening in their children in order to remind themselves of the revealed will of God for their kids' lives. For what we see now may be reality, but we must ask ourselves if it is truth according to God's Word.

Living prophetically means we become a "spokesman" to our family and speak words which at times may be corrective, but ultimately are always uplifting, comforting and encouraging. It means being aware of the times and seasons in which we live. The *Clock Father* constantly seeks to enable his children to see for themselves that God is about to call time on this earth[6] and that they should prepare to act accordingly. The Old Testament father Noah did that, as did Joseph, Jacob and a father called Issachar.

The children of Issachar "had understanding of the times, to know what Israel ought to do."[7] This *Clock Father* was so attune with God's timetable that he raised his children to not only understand the times they were living in, but what they should do about it. He created in each of his kids an ability to act as spiritual thermostats and become people who had a controlling influence on the world around them. These children became what Jesus talked about in the New Testament — "the salt of the earth" and "the light of the world."[8]

As a father, Issachar didn't just behave like some expert *time teller*; he *built clocks*. He didn't just chip away at their lives, shaping them as individual stones; he managed to set them into the grand scheme of world events. He didn't just keep the cogs running smoothly; he facilitated an environment in which the seeds of greatness could germinate and grow in each child. His kids could not only tell the times and seasons of God; they each had the ability to know what to do and to make a difference.

God said through His prophet Amos, "The Lord GOD does

nothing without revealing his secret to his servants the prophets."[9] One thing that means is we should sharpen our prophetic edge as fathers because parents are supposed to go before their children and make a way for them to follow.

What Clock Are You?

I believe that fathering can be characterized by various timepieces. If all dads were clocks, what kind of clock would you be?

Grandfather Clock.

The comforting ticktock of a *grandfather clock* is to me the best style of fathering. The dulcet tones of his hourly chimes, his prominent presence in the hallway, his tall long-case mahogany frame that proudly displays the craftsmanship of a master carpenter, the patina of longevity and a life well spent, the consistent regularity of his time-keeping are comforting and remind me that I'm home and all is well with the world.

Master/slave Clock.

For others, their preferred style of fathering might be more suited to the authoritarian characteristics of the *master/slave clock*. Public buildings and businesses widely used the slave clock in the nineteenth and early twentieth centuries: "[Slave clocks'] remote operation was regulated by electrical signals sent by a centralized master clock. These older styles of slave clocks either keep time by themselves, and are corrected by the master clock, or require impulses from the master clock to advance."[10] Similarly, *master/*

slave clock fathers exercise parental authority in a more autocratic way and have everyone calibrated to follow their lead to the split-second.

Without room for variation, deviation, creativity or individuality, their overbearing ways ignore the New Testament instruction we saw earlier, "Fathers, don't exasperate your children by coming down hard on them."[11] Demanding that others obey their lead to the letter, for them family life has been reduced to "What Dad says goes." With no room for discussion or debate, it's his way or the highway. Overriding the uniqueness in others, this "Simon Says" fathering style is an abuse of divinely delegated authority.

Cuckoo Clock.

Hidden for hours on end, the *cuckoo clock father*, like his counterpart, dutifully makes his theatrically styled appearance only periodically. Known for annoying the natives, his aggravating voice and regular flapping bouts only serve to make him feel good about himself, before recoiling back into his hideaway lifestyle. However, the reality of this style of fathering is a dusty relic of the past that only possesses a nuisance and noise factor that has little long-term value in building a strong Christian family.

Mantel Clock.

As the name suggests, for the *mantel clock father* it's all about insisting on a prominent position in the home that forces everyone else to look up to him. Struggling with a deep sense of insecurity, he must be the center of attention so as to find acceptance, appreciation and approval in how others see him. With his ornate facade and intricate dedication to detail, fathering is, for this guy, more about appearance than substance.

Stop Clock.

Never satisfied with his child's performance, the *stop clock father* merely marks a moment of success with an insignificant gesture, before continuing to push his young protégé to do better. Often living out his own failures through his children, the frustrated ego of the *stop clock father* is constantly dissatisfied with anything he or his children achieve, even though it might be their personal best. The mistake all stop clock fathers make is missing the unforgettable moments of today for the sake of something better tomorrow.

Alarm Clock.

While the whole household realizes the necessity of having them around, few can hide the fact that the piercing sound of the *alarm clock father* is both unwanted and unwelcome. Having the unenviable task of telling others what they don't want to hear, the "alarmist" father can become nothing more than a "striking hour dad" who insists on reminding others about their tardy lifestyle. Creating a kind of love/hate relationship with his children, the annoyance of this parenting style does little to bring about any long-term change, but, rather, creates a deep desire to "hit the snooze button" and go back to the way things were.

Valuable Timepiece

The truth is, the well-disciplined Christian family whose children jump into line when the *master clock* strikes time for church is one thing, but our purpose as fathers is to nurture our young people to become valued timepieces from which others take a reliable reading. While children need the influence of a male parent, the rare appearance of the *cuckoo clock father* whose flight of fancy, perpetual flapping and innocuous squawking all because something or someone has wound him up, does little to help. Neither does the overbearing prominence of the *mantle clock father* or the unrealistic expectations of the *stop clock father*. And, needless to say, the annoying and somewhat insensitive sound of the *alarm clock father* also does little to build the kind of legacy most fathers long to leave behind.

Of all these varied timepieces, the grandfather clock best depicts the *Clock Father*. Synchronizing his thoughts, words and actions with those of his eternal Father, somehow the presence of this type of dad in the home, like the grandfather clock, brings an air of comfort and reassurance. How our children need the comforting presence, reassuring sounds and reliable accuracy of the godly *Clock Father*! The outside world can be crazy, but a loving *Clock Father* brings a much-needed calming influence to his children.

Coming from a family of literal and behavioral clock makers (my grandfather was a watch case maker), everything in me over the years has shouted mechanical engineer/*time teller* father in that I want to organize my children's lives and set all in order for them. Perhaps somewhat late in the game, I've come to realize that my children are not pre-shaped cogs, nor are they robotic machines programmed to do what I think or what makes me feel good about myself. Children are tender plants that need to be nurtured and grow in an encouraging, comforting environment to become the best they can be. So if I were able to turn back the clock, I'd try much harder to be *a clock builder,* rather than a *time-teller.*

Getting in the Zone

My family lives in two different time zones. My wife and I live in the United States on Central Daylight Time (CDT) and our children all live in the United Kingdom on Greenwich Mean Time (GMT). While this might make life interesting, it also can prove to be challenging. They are six hours ahead of us, so our phone calls have to be carefully timed if we're not to wake a sleeping household or miss people altogether (like singing Happy Birthday to our children and grandchildren at 2 o'clock in the morning!). Yet while phoning can be inconvenient, it's nothing compared with the challenge of traveling to and from the U.S.

Soon after taking off from the Chicago airport, my first step to accepting the time difference is when I forward my wristwatch six hours to reflect Greenwich Mean Time. Although my body might take a while to adjust, my mind has to accept the fact that time has changed and I need to live accordingly. If I choose to ignore the time change and try for the whole duration of my trip to live on American time, problems will soon emerge. Missing prearranged appointments and the opportunities they present is one thing; being in the wrong place at the wrong time would more than likely ruin the whole purpose of the trip — all because I failed to live in the reality of a different time zone.

When it comes to *time*, the New Testament uses a couple of words to describe two very different and distinct "time zones." The Greek word *chronos*[12] is a word from which we get the English terms *chronometer* and *chronology*. The word *chronometer* appears on the dial of my forty-year-old wristwatch, so I know we're talking *clock* or *calendar time:* it's now 5:33 a.m. and it's the 24th of June 2009 — that's *chronos* time. The Bible also uses another word that has a totally different connotation in terms of time. The Greek word *kairos* speaks of a special moment that may or may not have anything to do with clock or calendar time,[13] and refers to kingdom time. One description of the difference in these two says:

"About nine months or so into a pregnancy — chronos time — many soon-to-be mothers shake their husbands by the shoulder and say, 'It's time!' He opens a bleary eye, looks at the clock, and says. 'It's 3:17 in the morning; go back to sleep!' She's on *kairos* time, but he's talking *chronos*. So he gets shaken again: 'It's time!' and this time he gets it! IT'S **TIME!!!!**"[14]

Some have even suggested that *kairos* time comes with an inbuilt idea of pregnancy. So when God talks time He's talking about something conceived in His own heart that will be birthed as and when He alone sees fit.

In the natural sense, the *Clock Father* will teach his child to read the time on a clock and the dates on a calendar. Yet few fathers understand the importance of enabling their children to move in tune with *kairos* or kingdom time.

Although we live in a time-space continuum that we respectfully obey, there is a system of time to which we all need to synchronize ourselves and make the most of the opportunities divinely afforded to us. While *chronos* time causes me to respectfully arrive on time for appointments, *kairos,* or kingdom time requires that I make those pre-arranged opportunities that God wants me or my child not to miss out on. Functioning as a *Clock Father* requires that I respectfully submit to both "time zones" and teach my children how to synchronize their lives to heaven's hourglass and not miss out on all that God has for them. As Solomon, possibly the wisest man who ever lived, said, "For everything there is a season, and a *time* for every matter under heaven."[15]

Working on His heavenly Father's timetable, Jesus often challenged His earthly parents with a role reversal that had Him helping them to understand kingdom time. When His mother asked Him to do something about the shortage of wine at the wedding at Cana, Jesus replied to her, "Woman, what does this have to do with me? My hour has not yet come."[16]

Although aware of *chronos* time, Jesus was a man working on two time zones, and *kairos* time took priority. Pregnant with the purpose of God, Jesus walked this life in perfect tune with His heavenly hourglass. Refusing to be pressured by people, objects or events that *chronos* time might demand, Jesus walked to the chime of a different clock.

In every godly father, there needs to be that same ability to know the times and seasons in which we are living, to live our *immediate* in the light of an *ultimate* — in order to create in our children the means to do the same.

Make the Most of Time

For over a quarter of a century, Dr. James Dobson of *Focus on the Family* fame has spoken prophetically and practically on issues of family life. A true *Clock Father*, he is someone who understands the times in which we live and what Christians should do. That's not surprising considering the *Clock Father*-like quality of his own dad.

A powerful preacher and successful evangelist, James Dobson, Sr. was, in his day, a man in great demand. Sought by churches throughout the United States for the purpose of evangelistic outreach, his calendar was fully booked four years out. His hectic schedule, however, meant that he often was away from his wife and family for long periods of time. In an effort to combat the challenge this created, the Dobsons devised a plan that would involve his being away preaching for two weeks and then home for two weeks, so he could help raise the family. For a while this worked well until one day while he was away on a two-week preaching trip he received a phone call from his wife asking for help.

Up to that point, his teenage boy, James, Jr., had been doing well at school and in sports, the Dobson marriage was good, and his ministry had taken off — but with that one phone call he realized there was trouble at home. Mrs. Dobson "had just had the latest in a series of arguments with their sixteen-year-old. She had asked him to do something and he told her point-blank that he wasn't going to do it. This six-foot-two boy was wearing her down. His strong will was starting to take its toll. So she called her husband and in a fairly short conversation reported the events that had just taken place. And simply said, 'I need you.'"[17]

According to *chronos* time, this dad could ill afford the time to stop what he was doing, but in tune with *kairos* time this was a moment he couldn't miss. Canceling his remaining meetings and clearing his calendar for the next few years, James, Sr. drove home. Within several days the house was on the market and he had secured the offer of a pastorate in another state.

For the next two years father and son teamed together for James, Jr. to finish school and enter college. Once that happened and his son was settled in a dorm, James, Sr. decided to re-engage in his former role as an evangelist — but things had changed. Many of his former contacts had retired and he had become relatively unknown to the new young pastors in his denomination. Although his time-out had cost him dearly, for him the price of making the most of the moment for the sake of his son's future was worth every sacrificial second. The legacy he left his son was priceless.

Recently, in a father's survey I asked a group of young men two questions about being a dad. Surprisingly the majority of answers were all around this issue of time. The answers most men gave to the first question, "Name your greatest failure as a father," were:

■ Not having enough time for my children.

■ Being too busy and not giving my children time.

■ Sometimes I let business and laziness get in the way of giving myself to my family.

■ Not spending the time with them that I'd like to.

■ Not spending enough time with my children, I missed out on so much.

In answer to the second question, "Name one piece of advice you'd give to young fathers," they responded:

■ Spend lots of time with your children.

■ Appreciate every stage of life, time passes all too quickly.

■ Don't just live for the moments but give all of yourself because today affects your tomorrow.

■ Spend as much time as possible with your children.

■ No job is worth sacrificing time with your children.

■ Spend quality time listening to your children.

While some may encourage fathers to give themselves to *quality* time as opposed to *quantity* time, given the choice, research shows that most children would always vote for more time with their dads.[18] What we might measure as poor quality is for them time they would much rather spend with you than anyone else. Children want to maximize every moment they can have with us, whether we're a resident or non-resident father. Dads should feel the same way about their kids.

One father I've heard of took his son to the playground and sat talking with a mom while their children played nearby. After awhile the dad told his son it was time to leave, but the boy pleaded with him for five more minutes, and the dad agreed. Shortly the father said to his son it was time to leave, and again the boy asked for five more minutes. When the dad said yes, the mother marveled at his patience — until he explained the source of it.

He told her that a year earlier his older son was riding his bike when a drunk driver hit and killed him. The father hadn't spent a lot of time with that son and now would give anything for just five more minutes with him. He vowed he would never make the same mistake with his younger son, so actually granting five more minutes of play gave the dad five more minutes with his boy.

Five minutes, five years, fifty years — we boast of what we plan to do tomorrow, but our tomorrows are never certain. So I encourage you as a dad to keep your eyes on the time, for life is short and the opportunities today affords you with your kids may not be here tomorrow. There's no such thing as a perfect father, but remember: "Life is a vapor, something that lasts for a short time. It is like an hourglass — it runs out; like a puff of smoke — it is there then it is gone. Live each day as if it is the last."[19]

Personal Reflections

• How would you describe your fathering style—John Humphrys style interviewer or stonemason; engineer or gardener; time-teller or clock builder?

• How would your children describe your words and actions to them? As the warm and friendly chime of a grandfather clock or the annoying noise of an alarm clock?

• Which time zone are you presently functioning in, *kairos* or *chronos,* and why? .

• What steps do you intend to take to improve on all these aspects of fatherhood?

 ## Group Discussion

Discuss with your group which of the various negative aspects of the timepieces outlined in this chapter you have at times struggled with and how you are seeking to live differently.

THE CHAMPION FATHER

No question about it, my dad is the Father of the Century!

—Richard Hoyt[1]

Determining to Be a Dad
Who Stands in the Gap

Hearing that his high school was planning a road race to raise money for a student paralyzed in an accident, Richard Hoyt shared with his dad how he would love to take part. Not the most athletic of fathers, Dick agreed to push his son for the whole five miles of the race. Ever since, Dick Hoyt has pulled, pushed and carried Richard in some of the most grueling sporting events known to man.

Richard suffered complications at birth that left him severely disabled. Yet it hasn't stopped this remarkable father/son team known as Team Hoyt from crossing the finish line of numerous activities that include 234 triathlons; 21 duathlons and 67 marathons.[2] This is not an easy exercise when you consider that to compete in the swimming leg of a triathlon, Richard gets to ride in a rubber boat which Dick pulls; for the bike riding part, Richard rides on a seat attached to handlebars as his dad peddles the bike; and for the running, Richard sits in a running chair that his dad has pushed to finish lines all across America.

Using a special computer by touching a switch with the side of his head, Richard shared his inner thoughts with his dad about that first race back in 1985. His response was encapsulated in a sentence he typed that read, "Dad, when we were running, it felt like I wasn't disabled anymore."[3] That one liner changed Dick Hoyt forever. Championing his son's cause, Dick became obsessed with giving Richard that feeling of freedom as often as he could.

Dick is someone who personifies the penultimate character of this book—the *Champion Father*. In the face of all opposing factors, champion fathers like Dick stand in the gap for their children so as to enable them to be the best they can be. Refusing failure as a viable option, they believe that, by God's grace, they and their children can make it to the finish line of every challenge in life.

By definition, a *champion* is someone who either "fights for a cause" or has "defeated the competition."[4] Therefore, becoming a *Champion Father* in the true sense of the word must involve our experiencing either *conflict* or *competition*. While most parents would love the opportunity to enjoy an environment where peace and partnership reign, the reality is, conflict and competition create the womb in which champions are conceived.

The Birthplace of Champions

In his book *The Time Machine,* H. G. Wells imagined a world free from weeds and fungi, where nettles didn't sting and summer evenings were mosquito-free. In this idyllic environment, everyone lived in splendid homes and wore expensive clothes, there was no such thing as social or economic struggle, and the necessity for work had been eliminated. Disease had been stamped out and people lived in perfect security in an earth where violence was rare. Yet in this somewhat utopian state, Wells observed that the removal of hardship, discomfort, conflict and competition had produced a weak, insipid, spineless generation. The weak remained weak and the strong had no need of their strength, resulting in a society that was physically, intellectually and emotionally crippled.

In the kind of world that Wells conceived, people became idle, easily fatigued, lacking in interest and quickly discouraged. That champions are birthed from the womb of conflict and competition is perhaps the reason why the apostle James wrote: "When all kinds of trials and temptations crowd into your lives...don't resent them as intruders, but welcome them as friends! Realize that they come to test your faith and to produce in you the quality of endurance."[5]

We can see the truth of this in the natural world. As the botanist watches the emerging caterpillar struggle from its chrysalis, he or she may be tempted to quicken the process by cutting the creature free. But, in those moments of greatest resistance, a secretion is released that strengthens and prepares the butterfly's wings for flight. Just as the caterpillar's struggle is essential to transform into a butterfly, the winepress is essential for producing wine, the crucible for purifying gold, the pruning hook for procuring the best fruit; so pressure, heat and loss are crucial for producing winners.

Capt. Charles (Chuck) Yeager hit major pressure and resistance just moments before he became the first man ever to break through the sound barrier. His plane began to vibrate violently; the shaking and pressure were so intense he believed he had only minutes to live. Some have even suggested that he radioed a message of love and farewell to his parents, as he waited for the inevitable. Having accepted the reality that his plane could disintegrate at any moment, he pushed through the brick wall into a realm that no other living person had ever reached. Had he backed off because of the intense pressure he was under, he might never have broken through the sound barrier and experienced flying at Mach 1.

All change is challenging. When babies pass through the birth canal, they experience pressure as part of their journey, the same way our children will have to face conflict and competitions en route to the winner's rostrum. Accepting this reality, the *Champion Father* walks his children through everyday hassles. Endeavoring to empower them to handle those people, objects and events that are an essential part of their ongoing development, he knows that winners have to face the trials of life before they can ever wear the garlands of success.

While none of us want to see our kids fight conflict or face competition, the reality is that these things are often the furnace in which champions are formed. A lack of challenging experiences will eventually cause problems for them.

No More Candy

Michael (not his real name) was an extremely angry young

college student whose violent outbursts were a constant concern to his parents. But on this occasion it was the air of finality in his voice during a Friday afternoon tutorial that caused his tutor concern. As they chatted, it soon became clear that Michael was preparing to cut all ties with his parents and leave home for good. With a vague notion that a friend in another city would offer him short-term accommodation, Michael had thrown all those family photos and personal mementos that could remind either him or his parents of his existence into the local river. He also had packed his bags and was ready to begin his new life.

Faced with an angry and somewhat desperate young man, the tutor recognized a camouflaged cry for help. Following a couple of quick phone calls, one to his wife and the other to the student's parents, it was agreed that Michael would stay at the home of his college tutor for a few days, before returning home. Well, that was the plan.

As days turned into weeks, it soon became apparent just how maladjusted Michael's life had become. For instance, at the meal table he would selfishly help himself to the majority of the food without any thought as to whether or not there was enough to go round. Then there was the occasion when in an act of Christian charity, his hostess kindly agreed to Michael's request to clean his shoes, only to have them returned the following morning with the complaint that there were still some spots of dirt on them. The final blow that sent Michael packing was the evening he kept banging on his hosts' bedroom door at 11:30 p.m. demanding he get up and taxi him to the local pizzeria to pick up his pizza. To us his behavior might seem somewhat bizarre, but to Michael it was normal everyday home life.

Amazed at their son's dysfunctional behavior and his decision to leave home for good, his parents just couldn't comprehend why he would do such a thing. "Why is he so angry with us?" they would constantly ask. *"We've done everything for him!"* Yet therein lay the root of Michael's problem.

His parents *had* done everything for their son, to the point of each night turning back the sheets on his bed. Candy coating Michael's life, they not only produced a fear in him that he would never be able to do anything for himself, they had inadvertently caused him to fall into the trap of entitlement. Believing that everyone owed him something, he had the misconception that life was all about him. These candy coating parents had suppressed his sense of self-worth and ability to handle life, and disabled rather than enabled him to live in the real world.

When parents allow their children to "run free in the candy store" without any sense of earning, we should expect the worst. People who fail to go through the forum of conflict or competition end up as adults who are often emotionally, socially and spiritually crippled. These individuals journey through life with an unhealthy attachment to their mother or father that can sometimes cause behavioral problems and marital pressures long after they've physically, but not mentally, left home.

The *Champion Father*, on the other hand, knows from personal experience that conflict and competition are the furnaces in which champions are forged. So he's willing to fight the fight and run the race for his kids' future.[6] If it means competing for his children's *time,* or *the right to be heard,* he'll do it. If he faces a conflict over our Christian *values,* he'll do battle for his kids in prayer—even if for awhile he has to suffer the pain of watching them sink deeper into the quagmire of differing social standards, because absolutes are no longer absolute and common-sense is no longer common.

Fathers must learn to fight with godly force for what they believe is right, rather than fold under the pressure of what they clearly know is wrong.

I believe that all fathers need to become spiritual warriors who avoid using natural strength, but choose rather to rely on the spiritual force invested in everyone who is born-again and filled with the Spirit. God's power resides on the inside of those of us who have received His Son Jesus as our Lord and Savior (have become born again), and received His Holy Spirit (have become filled with the Spirit). His power is known to have raised a dead child,[7] restored a demonized daughter,[8] returned a prodigal son,[9] *and is well able to change any situation we as modern-day fathers might have to face.*

Just as an ancient eastern shepherd would lie in the doorway of the sheepfold to form a physical door to protect the sheep, fathers need to fight (spiritually speaking) to keep destructive, negative influences from coming into their homes. This fight requires praying, believing and behaving like a winner, and placing their trust in a sovereign God who, in the face of all opposing factors, is able to overcome every obstacle and win.

Soar to New Heights

As a shepherd, the Old Testament character David would give chase after a predator rather than lose any of his sheep. Be it a lion or bear, he would fight to retrieve what had been taken.[10] The *Champion Father's* function is comparable in that he has a priestly role, standing in the gap for his children and, if and when necessary, aggressively fighting for their eternal welfare. Through prayerful intervention he too sets out to retrieve what has been lost.

Whether overseeing sheep, leading an army, or fathering a family, the nature of a champion is clearly seen in David, perhaps never more so than in the classic case of the Ziklag experience.[11] Not satisfied to sit back, settle for second best, and allow the circumstances of life to steal his family and get the better of him, David became righteously indignant over that case of daylight robbery by his enemy and fought for and retrieved what, as a father, was rightfully his.

Champion Fathers are godly dads who mediate, arbitrate and intercede on behalf of their children. They position themselves to spiritually bridge the gulf between the purpose of God and the plans of man, bringing about a godly resolve to every situation. Whether present or absent, these dads fight for their children's spiritual well-being. Using their fatherly prerogative, they approach the throne of grace on behalf of their kids through intercessory prayer—doing spiritual warfare against the enemy that threatens to rob each of them of their divine destiny.[12]

Let's face it, when it comes to fatherhood, trouble comes with the territory. As the biblical character Job once said, "Don't blame fate when things go wrong — trouble doesn't come from nowhere. It's human! Mortals are born and bred for trouble, as certainly as sparks fly upward."[13] Yet, not all conflict is necessarily a bad thing. Whichever way you cut it, *conflict*, linguistically as well as developmentally, has both a positive and negative side to it.

When the ancient Greeks used the word *conflict*, they pictured a sporting stadium in which they held their Olympian games, a place where competitors gathered and champions were ultimately recognized. The Latin word for *conflict* paints a picture of flint or iron being struck in order to produce a spark, which in turn produces fire as a source of heat and power. The Chinese, on the other hand, use two symbols for the same word, one meaning *danger* and the other *opportunity*. In all these word pictures we get the idea that *conflict* has both a negative and positive element: losers and winners, pain and gain, danger and opportunity.

At times our home might take on the appearance of a war zone — teenagers butting heads with parental authority, sibling rivalry, a hive of social activity where it seems more like a Roman amphitheater in which gladiatorial contests take place on a regular basis. However, *competition* (which we looked at in-depth in the first chapter) and *conflict* can prove to be a win-win for all concerned if the *Champion Father* sees them as an opportunity rather than an obstacle and handles them correctly.

Lovingly communicating the father heart of God in the midst of conflict is perhaps the hardest thing any father has to do.

No dad enjoys confrontation, but if our attitude is adversarial rather than redemptive, the outcome will always be disastrous. Some dads struggle with that because of having suffered from no fathering or negative fathering when they were kids, and they're still trying to put the shattered pieces together. Others are desperate to model something they believe their fathers failed to do. A mental attitude is made up of a set of *beliefs*, which may or may not be correct; it in turn affects our *behavior* and ultimately what we and those around us *become.* So fathers should first and foremost approach every situation with a right set of beliefs about God, ourselves and those with whom we are communicating.

Get our angle of approach wrong and relationships will crash and burn. If handled correctly, however, the hassles of life will help us soar to new heights of possibility together.

God or Godzilla?

In most Bible translations, the word *champion* is rarely used in scripture. Yet there seems to be an unusual concentration of the term in and around that historical fight between David and Goliath.[14] We're going to look at these two men because they offer great lessons for fathers to learn from on how we might become spiritual prize fighters and "fight the good fight of faith"[15] on behalf of ourselves and our families.

In every father there's a Goliath and David type conflict that wants to take charge in how we react or respond to a challenge. Although using different terminology, the apostle Paul echoes the same sentiments when he speaks about the wretched, carnal, old or natural Goliath-man present in all human beings, as something that conflicts with the new or spiritual David-man resident in all born-again believers.[16] Knowing that trouble will either bring the *best* or the *beast* out of us, we need to choose whether the way we are going to face challenges represents God or Godzilla.

The historian Josephus described Goliath as "a man of vast bulk, for he was of four cubits and a span in tallness."[17] Said by some to be 9 feet, 6 inches tall and weighing in at a possible 600 pounds, in the natural this Godzilla of a man used brute strength to win his battles and was not a fair match for a young teenager who possibly weighed less than Goliath's spear. In the case of fathers, some dads are no match for their children.

The Goliath-man father tends to resort to brute strength to win an argument. In the extreme, he is known to use mental, verbal and, sadly (and erroneously), even physical abuse to beat down the opposition. With a bark that is as big as his bite, Goliath-man is renowned for his shouting matches and male bravado. Goliath sought to intimidate the army of Israel by "strutting his stuff" around in the valley between them and "egging them on" to fight him, in an attempt to scare them into submission and ultimate surrender. In the same way the giant from Gath faced the Israelites, the Goliath-type father uses bully-boy tactics to produce fear, leaving his children feeling scared, inadequate and insignificant in his presence. While these tactics might, on the surface, win an occasional skirmish, in the long run they destroy relationships.

The David style of leadership is different. Rather than relying on brute force, David's strength came from his close relationship with God. Known as "a man after [God's] heart,"[18] David is an example of what the New Testament writer meant when he spoke of being "strengthened with power through his Spirit in your inner being."[19] David's true spirituality and power lay in his ability to allow God's Spirit to interact with his, so that he could do the right thing at the right time, in the right way.

Both of these men were considered to be champions by their nations, but out of an intimate relationship with his heavenly Father David was able to respond to conflict and competition in a godly way. Goliath intimidated people; David inspired them. Goliath produced insecurity, fear and feelings of insignificance; David created security, faith and a sense of significance in all who spent time with him. Which of these two would you say is the true champion?

The word *champion* speaks of physical might, but it also means "a man who stands in between."[20] David stood in the gap between the armies of Israel and the Philistines to intercede on behalf of his people. As gap-standing is associated with the priestly act of prayerful intercession, the *Champion Father* is willing to take on the opposition for the sake of his children, knowing that God Himself is searching "for a man…who should build up the wall and stand in the gap."[21]

Dick Hoyt stands in the gap between his ability and his son's disability. The biblical father of the returning prodigal[22] stood in the gap for the boy between home and the gauntlet of abuse that came from the oldest son. Jesus Christ stood in the gap between a righteous God and sinful humanity so as to make it possible for us to be in right relationship again with our heavenly Father.

The *Champion Father* is responsible to stand in the gap and help his kids to have a right relationship with him, as well as with God. That may sound easy, but it can be challenging and exhausting at times. If you are a father who's feeling the fatigue of a long protracted fight or even thinking that you've lost the battle, you might be ready to throw in the towel. Giving up is not an option for any dad in pursuit of the purpose of God.

"Commitment to the Commitment"

What the Masters is to golf, the Superbowl is to American football, and Wimbledon is to Lawn Tennis, the America's Cup is to yachting. The oldest active trophy in international sport, it predates the modern Olympics by forty-five years. Named after the first winning schooner, the trophy was by the American holders considered to be "their cup." Having successfully seen off all contenders for over a century, its loss to the *Australia II* in 1983 was for the New York Yacht Club a bitter pill to swallow. For USA skipper Dennis Conner, the 1983 defeat was doubly difficult to concede—having gained the privilege of representing his country, Conners became the first American yachtsman to lose the America's Cup since its inception in 1851.

Determined to right his wrong, Conners spent the next four years finding and training a crew suitable to regain the trophy and restore his country's yachting prowess. Seven days a week, up to eighteen hours a day, he prepared himself, his crew and his boat for the ultimate challenge. Searching for ten men from the hundreds available to him to create a crew of champions, he made it abundantly clear to all comers, "No one would make the team unless he put winning the cup ahead of everything else in life. You have to start with a goal, and then put everything else aside until you achieve it." With this kind of dedication in mind, Conners coined the phrase he deemed necessary to be a champion: *"A commitment to the commitment."*[23]

To Dennis Conner, taking part was never enough: that was merely a commitment. To be a winner required that these ten men were committed night and day to their initial commitment, and in 1987 it paid off—Dennis and his teammates won back the cup for America.

How much more do children need fathers who are willing to make that kind of lifelong commitment to fatherhood—guys who will not give up at the first sign of pressure or other more pleasurable pursuits, but will do whatever it takes to champion their children's purpose in life! Remember, it only takes a moment of passion to *become* a father, but it takes a lifetime of commitment to *be* one.

That kind of commitment will define you as a father *and* a man. So as one dad to another, I urge you to make "a commitment to the commitment" of raising your kids and to settle for no less than victory with each one. It will be extremely challenging, and at times even leave you feeling beleaguered and battle-scarred. But the rewards are enormous because it's a battle that will ultimately change the world—one child at a time.

Personal Reflections

If feedback is the breakfast of champions, let me encourage you to find a mentor with whom you can make yourself accountable regarding the following questions:

• In practical terms, how do you intend to stand in the gap to mediate, arbitrate and intercede for your children?

• Are you the type of father who tends to overly candy-coat the challenges your children need to face and, if so, what do you intend to do about it?

• When challenged, are you more Godzilla-like than God-like in your response? If the former, how do you intend to change?

• Is it possible that you have become somewhat overly cautious in your approach to fathering and you now tend to lay-up rather than going for the green of God's purpose for your children? What can you do instead?

 Group Discussion

Discuss ways in which, in the future, you plan to stand in the gap, face conflict and remain committed to the committment!

Chapter 11

THE
CAPTAIN
FATHER

In my class you can either call me Mr. Keating, or if you're slightly more daring, "O Captain! My Captain."

—John Keating (played by Robin Williams)

Dead Poets Society movie

Determining to Be a Dad
Who Steers a Straight and Steady Course

Without exception, all of the members of my family are film buffs, people who like nothing better than to exercise their cinematic expertise at various family gatherings. Mealtime conversations often consist of nothing more than a rally of film banter going back and forth across the dining table. Film nights are similar. Everyone has his or her own personal preference. While some insist that *Pride and Prejudice* get preferential treatment, others argue their case for another showing of the *Star Wars Trilogy* or the latest James Bond film. My personal preferences are *Mr. Holland's Opus* and *August Rush,* but my all-time favorite is *Dead Poets Society.*

In that piece of cinematic brilliance, Robin Williams plays the somewhat unorthodox prep school English teacher, Mr. Keating, who dared his students to call him "O Captain! My Captain!" in his attempt to broaden their horizons. Originating from a Walt Whitman poem of the same name, it's reckoned that the lines were probably written shortly after the assassination of

Abraham Lincoln and that the president is indeed the "Captain" of Whitman's creation. As an historic leader of a nation, who better to be called by that name than a man whose gentleness and strength in leadership were recognized as his greatest attributes? However, these are not reserved only for presidents. They reflect true values of fatherhood that should be seen in all whose children call them *Dad*.

One thing Lincoln and Keating have in common is that both men had passion: the President was passionate about helping his war-torn nation to heal; the English tutor was passionate about teaching his students life from a different perspective. Passion isn't prevalent in a lot of men nowadays. Once a Christian counselor was asked by well-known pastor and author Charles Swindoll, "What is the number one problem you face?" Without a moment's hesitation, the counselor replied, "Passive males!"[1] Absenteeism and abdication may be the reasons why many fathers fail to finish well, but apathy runs a close third, for when passivity overtakes passion the zeal of enthusiasm soon is extinguished.

Remember the Old Testament father named Eli? Suffering from a chronic attack of passivity, he failed to be passionate about his fathering responsibilities. Consequently, he didn't control or lay out boundaries for his wayward sons, nor did he "restrain"[2] them from displaying bad behavior.[3] He chose rather to verbally wrap their knuckles for being naughty boys. His inability to discipline his children had devastating results: not only did it contribute to a national disaster, but it directly resulted in his family losing their priestly heritage in the world and his two sons dying on the battlefield. Upon hearing the tragic news of the nation's defeat, the loss of the Ark of the Covenant and the death of his boys, this heavy, undisciplined, blind, impassive ninety-eight-year-old father fell backward off his chair and died from a broken neck — and in all probability a broken heart.[4]

When unruly children go ungoverned in the home, the ramifications are far reaching. For today's problem in the home is tomorrow's challenge in the school, workplace, playing fields and society as a whole.

Just how important is it to be passionate about raising our kids? It's been said that the Greeks never wrote an obituary for their fathers. They just asked one question of a man's life, "How much passion did he have?" In other words, how passionate was he in everything he said and did as a man? Did he give his all? Did he do his very best to be the kind of person life intended him to be? As a father, did his life reflect the true values of fatherhood? Was he someone on whom his children could rely to give them the support necessary to cross the finish line? Did he rule his moods, motives and mannerisms well? Did he take charge of all that was placed in his care? This isn't meant to condemn but to introduce important attributes of the final father character we're going to look at — the *Captain Father*.

I'm so glad that this was my own father's lifestyle. It's been said that the sum total of a person's life should be "to live, to love, to learn" and to be an example for others to follow.[5] That's how my dad lived. Tall, slim, and dignified, he exercised due diligence and dedication in all he did. Those who knew and loved him recognize that his example of honesty, respect, servant leadership, simple faith, hard work, excellence and passion for life are priceless characteristics to be admired and emulated. He always steered a straight and steady course. Catching the breeze of opportunity that took advantage of the winds of change, he sailed through life enjoying the ride. My dad was a *Captain Father* in the truest sense of the term.

The *Captain Father's* determination and ability to finish well and enable all his children to do the same is seen in the Hebrew word for *captain*, which has such meanings as "chief," "ruler," "keeper," "governor," "overseer" and "leader."[6] In a graphic sense, *captain* paints a picture of someone who exercises judicial justice, royal rule, military might. Whether the head of the courtroom, nation, army or tribe, this individual has one goal in life: to offer spiritual strategy, and guidance and direction to those in his charge.

This multifaceted type of dad takes charge of the children placed in his care and leads them by utilizing the nine fathering traits that have gone before this one. They all harmonize together and collectively form the *Captain Father,* which portrays the quintessential role of a godly dad. Simply put, to take charge as a *Captain Father* is to be in control of something or someone — in a healthy, positive way.

Who's in Control?

That God is in control can be seen throughout Scripture, but is never more evident than in the example of the Exodus found in the Old Testament. As "the captain of the LORD's host,"[7] God the Father successfully charted a course and led His kids (the children of Israel) into the Promised Land, a blessing that exceeded the present moment and has carried over for future generations to enjoy.

When speaking of God as *captain,* we're talking about our heavenly Father acting as a kind of head *teacher* overseeing his children's learning program; a *chieftain* who took charge of the needs of the tribe; a judge who gave words of wise counsel; a *leader* who governed well; and a *colonel-in-chief* who gave His "troops" a strategy to possess what was rightfully theirs. God steered His children in such a way as to confirm their potential in life, but He also clearly set borders and boundaries, rules and regulations that governed them — not to be cruel, hurtful or restricting, but to protect and bless them.

Like most boys I grew up with an insatiable desire for anything on four wheels. Born in the automobile capital of the United Kingdom, it was not surprising that if it moved mechanically it attracted my interest! In the accumulation of useless boyhood facts and figures, it was a known truth that, for anyone who managed to secure a government job and drive a company vehicle, speed was not going to be a factor. Whether a van, truck or car, these vehicles had all been duly doctored to limit their top speed. By applying some sort of gizmo to the acceleration mechanism, the ride was reduced to set the highest speed well below the vehicle's capability. This system of speed limitation was commonly known as a *governor,* an imposed rule that said to the driver, "this far and no further" — something Christian dads should be saying to their children on a regular basis.

By applying this concept to his family, a father establishes a level of kingdom rule that ensures his home will become an outpost of heaven on earth—an environment in which the principles of godly rule are known and followed by all who reside under his roof. The apostle Paul wrote about the benefits of utilizing this concept, and the consequences of not applying it, in a letter he penned to the Romans:

Throw yourselves wholeheartedly and full-time…into God's way of doing things. Sin can't tell you how to live…any longer. You're living in the freedom of God. … does that mean we can live any old way we want?… Hardly. …there are some acts of so-called freedom that destroy freedom. Offer yourselves to sin…and it's your last free act. But offer yourselves to the ways of God and the freedom never quits. All your lives you've let sin tell you what to do. But thank God you've started listening to a new master, one whose commands set you free to live openly in his freedom!… As long as you did what you felt like doing, ignoring God, you didn't have to bother with right thinking or right living, or right anything for that matter. But…where did it get you? A dead end. …now that you've…discovered the delight of listening to God telling you [what to do], what a surprise! *A whole, healed, put-together life right now, with more and more of life on the way!* Romans 6:13–22 MSG

Imagine what it would be like to live "a whole, healed, put-together life." Better yet, imagine giving that kind of life to your children. God's setting limits and establishing codes of practice and acceptable forms of behavior for all of His kids to obey were (and are) for their own good. The *Captain Father* follows in God's footsteps and, in a loving rather than legalistic manner, acts as an ambassador, governor or king of his family, saying to all who reside in his house, "This far and no further." Just as the first earthly father was given a garden to "keep it in order,"[8] so the modern father is required to exercise government over his "garden" and create a loving environment that will encourage the seeds of greatness to germinate and grow in each of his children.

Remember, though, that in order to function as the *Captain Father* and lead and govern others, we must take control of our own lives. We must first and foremost rule our own moods, motives and mannerisms before we can ever be judged worthy of exercising godly rule over others.[9] God divinely delegated parental authority, but those who refuse to "receive the abundance of grace and the free gift of righteousness...through the one man Jesus Christ"[10] and act as a true heavenly representative in the home risk opening the door for disorder or, worse, anarchy through personal abdication of rule. To set limits for our kids, then, we must be seen as men who set boundaries for ourselves — which can only be done by *leaning*.

Learning to Lean

Riding a classic 1966 BMW R60/2 motorcycle on the quiet back roads of America might for some be a dream, but to my wife it's a nightmare. Both of us first experienced the joy and horror of a power motorcycle by riding *pillion* or what our American friends prefer to call *passenger*. For me it was my brother, for Tina a former boyfriend, who first introduced us to the delights and dangers of motorcycle riding. Before ever being allowed to ride with my brother, however, he gave some sound advice as to how to ride as a pillion/passenger.

"When you sit behind me," he'd insist as only big brothers can, "you have to remember that when we take a corner, whichever way I lean you have to go with me. If you try to do your own thing and resist me, you'll not only make it hard for me to steer but the results could be disastrous."

That word *disastrous* was the one that got my attention. The bottom line to enjoying the ride was simple: Learn to lean.

The ride of fatherhood can end up disastrous too. So when it comes to ruling our thoughts, words and emotions, we as fathers need to learn how to lean on our heavenly Father, or as the biblical Proverb puts it, "Trust in the Lord with all your heart, and do not lean on your own understanding."[11] You see, leaning on God involves going with His grace — that divine ability of God that enables us to do what we can't do on our own. The grace of God is His undeserved, unconditional love and acceptance that's available to all those who believe, and it's vital.

We've talked a lot about grace already, and with good reason: It is the foundation of this message, for being a good dad is not hard — it's impossible on our own! We must learn how to lean on God. We do that by daily calling on Him through prayer, Bible reading, and quiet meditation on Scripture. *Leaning* is basic to enjoying the ride we call *fatherhood*. Like the apostle Paul, all fathers should say, "By the grace of God I am what I am."[12]

At times my own attempts at fathering were poor and somewhat shabby and pitiful. Once I began to fully understand the importance of leaning, I realized that the only way I can possibly reign over my mood swings, my tendency to react rather than respond, and my tendency to give people a look that kills or the silent treatment was to learn how to lean. In other words, I had to "receive the abundance of grace" so as to "reign in life through the one man Jesus Christ."[13] If we don't lean on God, we'll lean on someone or something else — with devastating effects.

Mary's Story

Although the advertisement simply read, "Gary,[14] please come home, your family needs you," it hid the reality of a dad who had disappeared some weeks earlier and was about to miss the birth of his fifth child. Coming into the world with a dad who couldn't even be bothered to be around for her birth, Mary,[15] now a middle-aged woman, still struggles with this nonexistent father/ daughter relationship. Possessing only two photographs of her childhood that include both her and her father, she writes, "I have no recollection of my dad's endearment. He was obsessed and in love with Kessler whisky and Budweiser beer. Everything he did revolved around drinking...always standing up for the underdog and friendly with visitors, he did all of it with a drink nearby.

"I did learn to be quiet at the table, to drink my milk and not spill it, speak respectfully to elders, and finish everything on my plate, but all without a dad/daughter relationship. Suffering from the advanced stages of alcoholism, Dad was drunk at my 18th birthday party and drunk when he walked me down the aisle."

As a dedicated Christian, Mary is learning how to lean on the grace of God for her daily support and, although she may still hobble a little, she is determined that, by God's grace, she will make it to the finish line and say with Paul, "I have fought the good fight, I have finished the race, I have kept the faith."[16] Like so many, Mary continues to fight the demons created by a previous chapter of her family history that has inadvertently become a part of her own ongoing story.

Again and again in researching this book, I've heard the sad tales of woe from children whose lives have been turned from a classic love story into a Greek tragedy by scary antics of their dysfunctional, drunkard, disappearing or divorced fathers. For some unfathomable reason, these guys actually believe that the results of their actions would be solely heaped on their own heads; that with their passing, all consequences would cease. How wrong can a father be?

Making a Positive Contribution

William Shakespeare may have said, "All's well that ends well," but one only has to look at the long list of biblical characters to realize that it's not always true. Stumbling over several common obstacles, most of the people who fail to cross the finish line do so because they have either forgotten the importance of a strong personal relationship with God or the need to daily feed a godly vision of who they are in Christ, His Son. For others, it's an inability to turn mistakes into learning opportunities or to maintain a godly character in the face of all opposing factors.

Perhaps the one common denominator in all who fail to finish well is the absence of what might be called a *contribution mindset:* to go through each day with a sense that how we choose to live our lives will undoubtedly have a direct bearing on how our kids live theirs.

As Christian men we understand the truth that God "has put eternity into man's heart,"[17] but we must seek to live with an unconventional perspective that exceeds this present moment. Read the life story of any godly man and you will see someone who lived their days with an eternal, rather than temporal mind-set. Living their immediate in the light of an ultimate, they watched what they said and didn't say, what they did and didn't do, knowing that one day they would have to give an account[18] for the kind of life they have lived. Eternity will reflect how we handled the role of fatherhood and what we did with the time, energy and resources God made available to us. So, living with an eternal contribution mind-set should change what we believe and challenge the way we behave, as ultimately it will determine what we become.

Your father may have left you zero in terms of a positive contribution, yet it's within the realm of possibility for each one of us to break the cycle and write a new chapter that will change the genre of our children and our children's children.

Whether history remembers us for what we *manufacture, model, mentor, minister, mention, master or mission* in our lifetime, we will all be remembered for something. Every one of us will make a contribution to the next generation. The question is—will our being here be viewed as a blessing or a curse?

In the movie *Dead Poets Society*, John Keating took his English students out of the classroom and into the lobby on the first day of class. A prestigious prep school based on *tradition, honor, discipline* and *excellence*, this was not a place that accepted change easily. To help his class get a different perspective on life he focused their attention on the photos of former graduates so as to consider the concept of *Carpe Diem* (Latin for "seize the day"[19]). In this, Keating began to *captain* his class and lead his students on an expedition of literary enterprise that had them tearing pages out of books, standing on desks, shouting a barbaric "*Yawp,*" and daring to address their literary leader as "O Captain! My Captain!"

In the closing scene, the dismissal of Keating is marked by an unconventional gesture of respect from his students. Having been forced to resign his post as tutor due to his avant-garde teaching methods, he enters his classroom to collect some personal belongings. His final departure from the room stirs memories of greatness in his former pupils, who take it upon themselves to stand on their desks to acknowledge his ability to teach them life from a different perspective. Forming a verbal guard of honor, one by one they each declare those four fabulous words, "O Captain! My Captain!" to which Keating responds with thanks.

When the final scene of life is played out and this *Captain*

Father exits the room for the last time, it's my dream to have my children mark my passing, in essence, with the unconventional desk-standing exercise that applauds my accomplishment as a great tutor who endeavored to give them a higher perspective on life and mark my departure with the proud words, "O Captain! My Captain." I believe that deep down in their hearts this is what all fathers want and strive for – to finish the race and hear their children voice their recognition of a job well done. Yet it's reciprocal. Their children hope they, in turn, will hear the faint echoes of their dads lovingly responding as Keating did: "Thank you, boys, thank you."

Determined to Finish the Race

The year was 1992; the occasion the Olympic Summer Games in Barcelona, Spain; the event, a qualifying heat for the men's 400 meters final. Having been forced, ten minutes before the race, to withdraw from the same event at the 1988 Olympics in Seoul, Korea with an Achilles tendon injury, Derek Redmond had missed his opportunity for a medal. He later had to undergo numerous surgeries to repair his injury, and the road to recovery had been an arduous one. Derek worked hard for the chance to represent his country at Barcelona. But this was no time to look back; he needed to finish this race as one of the four fastest qualifiers to give himself a fighting chance at an Olympic gold.

As always, Derek's father had accompanied him to the event for, whether on or off the track, these two were inseparable. Although his son's best friend, Jim Redmond had for now to be satisfied with taking his seat among the spectators high up in the stands only to watch Derek settle himself into the starting block and wait for the race to begin.

With the sound of the starting gun still ricocheting around the stadium, Derek took off in an all-out bid to make it through to the Olympic final of the men's 400 meters. Quickly reaching his stride, the dream of a place in the final was moving from possibility to reality with every meter he ran. A gold medal opportunity was the furthest from his mind; he just wanted a chance to run in the final. Running down the back straight and gaining on the opposition, he had only 175 meters to the finish line when suddenly disaster struck. Hearing a pop in his right hamstring, he was literally stopped in his tracks. Pulled up lame, his running stride was quickly reduced to hobble before eventually collapsing to the ground.

Convinced that the best British hope for a men's 400 meter gold medal was finished, the television broadcasters yelled repeatedly, "Derek Redman is out of the race!" Taken up with the remaining runners, the cameras stayed fixed on the race as each of the competitors made it to the finish line. Only when the race was finally won did the director decide to pull the cameras back to where Derek was trying to pull himself up from the ground.

In a moment Derek Redmond slowly began to rise to his feet and set off hobbling along the track. The mental and physical agony clearly visible on his tear-soaked face, the young man was determined to finish his race and nothing and no one was going to stop him. Refusing all offers of help, he slowly began to head toward the finish line. When the crowd realized what this seemingly failed runner was attempting to do, they began to stand and cheer him on with shouts of encouragement, but Derek would later report, "I wasn't doing it for the crowd. I was doing it for me. Whether people thought I was an idiot or a hero, I wanted to finish the race."[20]

A lone figure limping along the track in front of a crowd of 65,000 spectators, Derek had no idea that his father had already left his seat and had made his way as fast as he could to the edge of the track. Climbing the perimeter fence and brushing aside guards and track officials, Jim somehow managed to make it to his son's side. Recognizing his dad's friendly face, Derek threw his arm around his father to gain moral and physical support, as together they made their way toward the finish line.

For years, Jim had been at his son's side, getting up in the early morning hours for practices, encouraging, supporting and cheering him on. Now, in one last ditch effort this dynamic duo determined to do whatever it took to make it to the finish line and finish what together they had started.

Sometimes, life as a father gets ugly. Failure seems to frame those experiences in which the stress and tension of everyday life have resulted in a torn relational ligament. Although we entered this fathering event with high hopes of finishing well, a breakdown in communications has pulled us up lame. Struggling to make any headway, we attempt to hobble along for a while, but eventually the anguish and pain of a severed relationship becomes too much to handle and we collapse to the ground in a hopeless heap.

Harboring an overwhelming desire to give in to the pain and give up on the goal of finishing what we began, failed fathers run the risk of joining the ranks of thousands of "wannabe" dads who once ran well. Having messed up or missed out on our chance to be there for our children, the thought of blowing a once-in-a-lifetime opportunity is often enough to cause the strongest dad to leave the field of play.

Yes, we may feel hamstrung in our relationships with our children and we may be hobbling around the track just trying to make it to the finish line, *but we were never intended to run this race alone.* Our heavenly Father is seated in the stands, surrounded by thousands of former runners, "veterans cheering us on."[21] And, having seen us fall, He wants to come alongside to give us a strong shoulder to lean on, an offer of moral, physical and spiritual strength to finish our race.

All I can say is — *Take it.* For if, as fathers, we have any hope of making it to the finish line, it will only be by learning to lean on the grace of God. As one of the few biblical leaders who finished well and could say, "I have finished the race,"[22] the apostle Paul concluded, "But by the grace of God I am what I am, and his grace toward me was not in vain."[23] In so doing, God Himself will enable us not only to make it to the finish line of every challenge we face as dads, but to shoulder the challenges our children might face in life, as well.

In that one memorable Olympic moment, Jim Redmond became the epitome of everything this book has tried to portray about true fatherhood. The *Cavalier, Coach, Cheerleader, Compass, Companion, Composer, Cinderella, Clock,* and *Champion Father* culminating in the *Captain Father* — we see them all in this one supreme sacrificial act of a dedicated dad. To do whatever it takes to enable your child to be the best they possibly can be, no matter what their disability; to position yourself in such a way as to empower them to run their race, and to do whatever fair, positive, godly measures it takes to get them across the finish line — that is the true essence of fatherhood.

Personal Reflections

Considering the ten characteristics of fatherhood covered in this book, rate your strengths and weaknesses in each area on a scale of 1 to 10—with 10 being exceptional and in no way could be improved, and 1 being incredibly bad and in need of help.

• **The Cavalier Father**—makes a way in which his family can safely follow his lead, knowing that he is always looking out for them.
Circle one: 1 2 3 4 5 6 7 8 9 10

• **The Coach Father**—leads his children in a way that lovingly encourages them to be the best they possibly can be.
Circle one: 1 2 3 4 5 6 7 8 9 10

• **The Cheerleader Father**—speaks words of encouragement to his children at every given opportunity.
Circle one: 1 2 3 4 5 6 7 8 9 10

• **The Compass Father**—lives the kind of life from which his children can always be sure to take a good bearing in things spiritual, educational, financial, social and physical.
Circle one: 1 2 3 4 5 6 7 8 9 10

• **The Companion Father**—refuses to allow his children to feel they are journeying through life unaccompanied; he stays with them through the highs and lows of life.
Circle one: 1 2 3 4 5 6 7 8 9 10

• **The Composer Father**—seeks to enable his children to resonate their own song with the praises of heaven, be it through melodious words, a beautiful painting, a gorgeous smile or some other inherent ability.
Circle one: 1 2 3 4 5 6 7 8 9 10

• **The Cinderella Father**—lives the kind of life that deals with regret and remorse in such a way as to inspire others to do the same.
Circle one: 1 2 3 4 5 6 7 8 9 10

• **The Clock Father**—speaks God's prophetic word into the home in a timely manner and endeavors to "build clocks" rather than merely "tell time."
Circle one: 1 2 3 4 5 6 7 8 9 10

• **The Champion Father**—takes on competition and conflict, and also stands in the gap to intercede, mediate and arbitrate on behalf of his children.
Circle one: 1 2 3 4 5 6 7 8 9 10

• **The Captain Father**—rules himself and his circumstances in such a way that enables him to govern and bring order to his home, and set limits as needed.
Circle one: 1 2 3 4 5 6 7 8 9 10

 Group Discussion

Pick the most prominent of your successes in the above characteristics and share with the group the story of how, leaning on the grace of God, you managed to hobble across the finish line on a particular occasion.

CONCLUSION

Writing a book on any subject can be highly dangerous because people immediately consider you to be an expert. In my case nothing could be further from the truth. No matter how neat, nice and near-perfect everyone else seems to you, take it from me, appearance is deceptive. The façade may look good, but most fathers struggle with feelings of failure.

Fully expecting their end of term report to read, "Tries hard, but could do better," the last thing dads want to hear is the obvious. So, if, as a father, you feel you could have done better, that you've possibly blown the one opportunity to be "Super Dad," that given your time over you'd do things differently, then welcome to the Association of Imperfect Fathers.

As a fully paid-up member, I know one thing: When I eventually stand before my Maker, He won't ask for the family photo I carry in my wallet. Totally aware of my imperfections, all my heavenly Father will want to know is did I do everything I could to be the best father I possibly could be?

Fatherhood is a challenge at the best of times and, like most dads, I've made my fair share of mistakes. If time travel were an option, I would love to go back and visit that twenty-five-year-old kid (me!) who is about to make his first of four trips to the delivery room and get him to read these ten characteristics of highly effective fathering. In this way, I would hope to help him understand some of the things I've either stumbled on or searched for in nearly forty years as a dad:

■ While others *muddle through,* he makes a way — the *Cavalier Father.*

■ While others *magnify the problem,* he sees a solution — the *Coach Father.*

■ While others *mumble their thoughts,* he shouts words of encouragement — the *Cheerleader Father.*

■ While others *send mixed messages,* he gives clear direction — the *Compass Father.*

■ While others *migrate,* he stays close — the *Companion Father.*

■ While others *mess up,* he makes music — the *Composer Father.*

■ While others *muse on their mistakes,* he seizes the opportunity — the *Cinderella Father.*

■ While others *mistake the time,* he maximizes the moment — the *Clock Father.*

■ While others *master the charade,* he makes a difference — the *Champion Father.*

■ While others *memoir the past,* he makes history — the *Captain Father.*

Conclusion

Who is he?

*He's the imperfectionist in all of us who are fathers...*the dad who knows that while God is willing to forgive and forget our moods, mistakes, or misdemeanors for which we are truly repentant, it's only by His grace that any of us can become the kind of father we long to be. Who is that? Someone our children can trust as a confidante, ally and friend who stands in the gap, fights for a cause and competes for an incorruptible prize—the godly path our children's lives will follow. Perhaps this final story sums it up best.

Who's Flying Your Plane?

As the commercial flight suddenly dropped several hundred feet on a turbulent roller-coaster ride from Los Angeles to New York, a frightened gentleman frantically shredded yet another tissue in a vain effort to calm his nerves. Visibly shaken by the whole scary experience, he found little comfort in the fact that the unaccompanied child sitting next to him seemed totally unfazed by the whole event.

Oblivious to the turbulence that was causing some passengers to brown bag what remained of their lunch, the young girl continued to play with her electronic game. With his inquisitive mind beginning to get the better of him, the frantic man felt he had no option but to inquire as to what the young girl's secret was.

"Aren't you scared?" he asked.

"No," she replied.

How a young girl flying unaccompanied could remain so calm

in the middle of a storm like this was beyond him; so, desperate for answers, he inquired, "Why not?" to which the little girl answered, "Because my dad's flying the plane!"

Let me ask you one simple but all-important question: Who's flying your plane? To only *service* the needs of those on board your "flight" is not enough. You must *take your place* on the flight deck and *pilot* your family through the turbulent as well as the tranquil, times in a way that you all can reach your divine destiny. That requires faith and leaning on the grace of God.

Be it a mystery, thriller, comedy, love story or work of sheer fiction, your story as a father is but a chapter in the annals of your family's history, a scene in a theatrical performance in which your children's lives will follow. How you choose to live your chapter, your act, your time, will undoubtedly have a direct bearing on how they live theirs. And that is the whole reason for this book.

As a dad you are the father of one or more unique, irreplaceable, wonderful people who will enrich your life beyond measure and afford you the opportunity to enrich theirs. Your role as a father may have been a breeze up to now, or it may seem as if it's fraying around the edges and about to fall apart at the seams. What I have candidly, empathetically and humbly written in these pages is meant to be a kind of footprint in the sand to help and encourage you — and *through you* encourage your children — to live extraordinary lives for a cause and power bigger than yourselves.

About the Author

Photo by Hannah Reid (www.hannahreid.com)

Chris Spicer lives with his wife, Tina, in America's Midwest where he is presently serving as Teaching Pastor for Riverside Community Church, a large charismatic church in Peoria, Illinois. He also has been employed as a carpenter, businessman, senior pastor, teacher and Bible college principal, but he is, first and foremost, a husband, father and grandfather.

No Perfect Fathers Here is his third publication and was born out of his last book entitled, *Trust God & Keep Your Powder Dry,* which was semi-autobiographical and written for an audience of four. That book outlined the grace of God in his family over the last hundred years and was a Christmas 2008 gift to each of his four children. It soon became the inspiration behind *No Perfect Fathers Here,* which was written for a much wider audience of dads, would-be-dads, single dads, step-dads, separated dads, granddads and great granddads everywhere.

He and Tina presently reside in Peoria, Illinois, USA, while his four amazing adult children and four wonderful grandchildren live in the United Kingdom.

Other Books by Chris Spicer

VIII Characteristics of Highly Effective Christians

Trust God & Keep Your Powder Dry

Endnotes

Introduction

[1] 1 Corinthians 15:10.

[2] Matthew 13:44 MSG.

Chapter 1

[1] Bill Cosby, *Fatherhood* (New York: Berkeley Publishing Group, 1987), 18.

[2] Martin Luther King, Jr., *The Autobiography of Martin Luther King, Jr.* (New York: Grand Central Publishing, 2001), 4–5.

[3] *Shorter Oxford English Dictionary*, available from http://www.askoxford.com/concise_oed/father?view=uk, s.v. "father."

[4] *Merriam-Webster's Online Dictionary*, available from http://www.merriam-webster.com/dictionary/father, s.v. "father."

[5] *Noah Webster's Dictionary of American English*, available from http://www.e-sword.net/dictionaries.html, s.v. "father."

[6] *Collins Family Dictionary* (New York, NY: Harper Collins Publishers Limited,1999), 272, s.v. "father."

[7] Bill Cosby, 38.

[8] Psalm 127:3 MSG.

[9] American term for the English word *tap*.

[10] 2 Corinthians 10:12–18.

[11] 2 Timothy 4:7 KJV.

[12] Hebrews 12:1.

[13] 1 Samuel 17:38–39.

[14] Psalm 139:13.

[15] 1 Samuel 17:34–36.

[16] Zechariah 4:10 NCV.

[17] Hebrews 12:1–2.

Chapter 2

[1] Steve Farrar, Point Man—*How a Man Can Lead His Family* (Sisters, OR: Multnomah Books, 1990), 17.

[2] T.J. McGinley, *Ghost Warriors*, article available from http://www.327infantry.net/node/3187.

[3] 1 Corinthians 11:14.

[4] C.W. Slemming, *Made According to Pattern* (Ft. Washington, PA: CLC Publications, 2007), 27.

[5] Exodus 32:1 NKJV; Deuteronomy 1:30.

[6] *BBC News*, "Lorenzo's Oil: The Full Story," available

from http://news.bbc.co.uk/2/hi/health/3907559.stm.

[7] Arthur Blessitt, *The Cross* (Colorado Springs, CO: Authentic Publishing, 2009) back cover.

[8] Faith Popcorn, *The Popcorn Report*, Harper Business, 1992, 27.

[9] Deuteronomy 32:11–12.

[10] Luke 10:25–37.

[11] Julian Fulbrook, *Outdoor Activities, Negligence and the Law* (Farmham, Surrey, UK: Ashgate Publishing, 2005), 40.

[12] Romans 12:2 PHILLIPS.

[13] UNICEF, "Goal: Reduce Child Mortality," available from http://www.unicef.org/mdg/childmortality.html; also the World Bank Group Annual Report, 2004, available from www.worldbank.org.

[14] Brian Blessed wrote these words (which he accredited to George Mallory) to me in a copy of his book that I had purchased at a book signing event held for him.

[15] Richard Paul Evans, *The Five Lessons a Millionaire Taught Me About Life and Wealth* (Whitby, Ontario, Canada: Fireside Publishing, 2005), 69.

[16] This is not referring to the natural world, but many worldly systems are a front for demonic activities.

Chapter 3

[1] Carey Casey with Neil Wilson, *Championship Fathering* (Carol Stream, IL: Tyndale House Publishers, 2009), xiv.

[2] Based on a definition from *Merriam-Webster's Online Dictionary*, available from http://www.merriam-webster.com/dictionary/magnum%20opus, s.v. "magnum opus."

[3] Psalm 127:3 MSG.

[4] Psalm 139:14 KJV.

[5] Psalm 139:13 MSG

[6] Job 10:11–12.

[7] Ravi Zacharias, *The Grand Weaver* (Grand Rapids, MI: Zondervan, 2007), 24–25.

[8] Based on information from Thayer and Smith, *The KJV New Testament Greek Lexicon*, "Greek Lexicon entry for Poikilos," available from http://www.biblestudytools.com/lexicons/greek/kjv/poikilos.html, s.v. "varied, manifold," 1 Peter 4:10.

9 Ephesians 6:4.

10 Based on information from Thayer and Smith, "Greek Lexicon entry for Paideia," available from http://www.biblestudytools.com/lexicons/greek/kjv/paideia.html, s.v. "nurture" (KJV), "discipline," Ephesians 6:4.

11 1 Timothy 4:7.

12 Based on information from Thayer and Smith, "Greek Lexicon entry for Gumnazo," available from http://www.biblestudytools.com/lexicons/greek/kjv/gumnazo.html, s.v. "exercise" (kjv), "train," 1 Timothy 4:7.

13 See Luke 2:52.

14 Proverbs 27:17.

15 Genesis 18:19; Exodus 12:26–27; Deuteronomy 4:9; 6:7.

16 Michael Ray King, "Fathers, Encourage Your Children," available from www.ezinearticles.com.

17 Deuteronomy 6:7 MSG.

18 Proverbs 22:6.

19 Proverbs 22:6 MSG.

20 Isaiah 55:8.

21 Proverbs 22:6 KJV, marginal reference of my mother's old Authorized King James Bible, published by Collins' Clear Type Press.

Chapter 4

1 Mark de Rond, The Last Amateurs: To Hell and Back with the Cambridge Boat Race Crew (London, Great Britain: Icon Books, 2008), taken from dust cover of the book.

2 Ibid., 9.

3 Mark Davies, "Little Things Count," BBC Sport, March 19, 2004, available from http://news.bbc.co.uk/sport2/hi/other_sports/boat_race_2004/3523858.stm, s.v. "Boat Race 2004."

4 See 2 Timothy 4:7.

5 Job 38:7 MSG.

6 See Luke 2:13–14; 15:10.

7 Joshua 6:1-21.

8 Hebrews 12:1 MSG

9 Matthew 3:17.

10 Mark 9:7; Luke 9:35.

11 1 Thessalonians 2:11 MSG.

12 U.S. Department of Health and Human Services (HRSA), "Program Assistance Letter: Understanding the Health Care Needs of Homeless Youth," available from http://bphc.hrsa.gov/policy/pal0110.htm.

13 Cherry Norton, Social Affairs Correspondent, "100,000 children run away from home every year," The Independent (newspaper), available from http://www.independent.co.uk/news/uk/home-news/100000-children-run-away-from-home-every-year-744016.html.

14 Luke 15:11–32.

15 Ephesians 6:4 AMP; Colossians 3:21.

16 Ephesians 4:26.

17 Colossians 3:21.

18 Colossians 3:21 AMP

19 Luke 24:13–35.

20 Colin Brown, ed., Dictionary of New Testament Theology, Vol. 1 (Grand Rapids, Michigan: Zondervan Publishing House, 1980), 569.

21 Rick Reilly, "On Top of the World," Sports Illustrated, available from http://www.sportsillustrated.cnn.com/2006/magazine/06/26/where.norman.

22 Rick Reilly, Sports Illustrated, Dec. 30, 1966–Jan. 6, 1997 issue, 66.

23 Michael Ray King, "Fathers, Encourage Your Children," Fatherhood 101: Bonding Tips for Building Loving Relationship; see ezinearticles.com.

24 Mark 5:24–34; Matthew 9:18–26; 14:36.

25 To safeguard this person we have changed his name to John.

26 Denzel Washington, A Hand to Guide Me (Des Moines, IA: Meredith Books 2006), 8.

Chapter 5

1 Genesis 5:22.

2 Paula Wolfson, Jewish Fathers: A Legacy of Love (Woodstock, VT: Jewish Lights Publishing, 2004) 6.

3 James 1:17.

4 A relationship with God begins with spiritual birth and grows by means of spiritual disciplines such as daily Bible reading and time spent alone with Him, talking to Him.

5 The scriptwriters of the film Apollo 13 deliberately changed the quote so that it

appeared something was happening in the present rather than the past, having the actor Tom Hanks say "Houston, we *have* a problem."

⁶ Drs. Henry Cloud and John Townsend, *Boundaries Workbook* (Grand Rapids, MI: Zondervan, 1995), 7.

⁷ Dr. Henry cloud, Dr. John Townsend, *Boundaries with Kids* (Grand Rapids, MI: Zondervan, 1998), 16.

⁸ Deuteronomy 19:14; 27:17; Proverbs 22:28; 23:10; Job 24:2.

⁹ See Joshua 19:11, 22, 26, 27, 34 KJV. In verse 11, the Hebrew word *paga* is translated as "reach to," from which we get the English word *intercession*. This is based on information from Brown, Driver, Briggs and Gesenius, *The KJV Old Testament Hebrew Lexicon*, "Hebrew Lexicon entry for Paga," s.v. "reached to," Joshua 19:11.

¹⁰ Matthew 25:14–30.

¹¹ Matthew 5:37

¹² Genesis 5:22.

¹³ Exodus 4:22; Deuteronomy 8:5 MSG.

¹⁴ Brown, Driver, Briggs and Gesenius, "Hebrew Lexicon entry for Yacar," available from http://www.biblestudytools.com/lexicons/hebrew/kjv/yacar.html s.v. "discipline," Deuteronomy 8:5 MSG.

¹⁵ Only 39 times in the Old Testament.

¹⁶ See Deuteronomy 32:6; 2 Samuel 7:14; 1 Chronicles 28:6; Psalm 68:5.

¹⁷ 1 Corinthians 10:11 NASB.

¹⁸ Michael Gurian, *The Purpose of Boys* (San Francisco, CA: Jossey-Bass, 2009), 122.

¹⁹ Ibid., 121.

²⁰ Brown, Driver, Briggs and Gesenius, "Hebrew Lexicon entry for Midbar," available from http://www.biblestudytools.com/lexicons/hebrew/kjv/midbar.html, Strong's #4057, s.v. wilderness."

²¹ Exodus 25: 8, author paraphrase.

²² Exodus 3:8.

²³ Quote available from http://awsimx.fathermag.com/Feature-Stories-Dads.shtml.

²⁴ See Psalm 136 NASB.

²⁵ Deuteronomy 8:1–5.

²⁶ See Exodus 14.

²⁷ 1 Corinthians 13:4–7 MSG.

²⁸ 1 John 4:7–8, 16.

²⁹ Hebrews 12:4–11 MSG.

³⁰ Proverbs 14:12.

³¹ Romans 3:23.

³² John 14:6.

³³ Charles W. Colson, *Born Again* (Ada, MI: Chosen Books, 1976), 5.

³⁴ Jonathan Aitkin, *Chuck W. Colson: A Life Redeemed* (WaterBrook Press, 2005), 528.

³⁵ Matthew 5:1–12.

³⁶ Edited by Cook Communications, *Fathers of Influence* (Colorado Springs, CO: Honor Books, 2006), 85.

Chapter 6

¹ Max Lucado, *In the Grip of Grace* (Nashville, TN: W Publishing Group, 1996), 181–184.

² Genesis 2:18 MSG.

³ 1 Thessalonians 2:11–12 MSG.

⁴ Barack Obama, *Dreams from My Father* (New York, NY: Crown Publishers, 2007), 3.

⁵ Armin A. Brott, *Father for Life* (New York, NY: Abbeville Press, 2003), 45–46.

⁶ Based on information from www.vocabulary-lesson-plans.com/prefix-com.html and www.merriam-webster.com/dictionary/companion, s.v. "companion."

⁷ Matthew 26:26; 1 Corinthians 11:23–24

⁸ Stephen R. Covey, *The 7 Habits of Highly Effective Families* (London, UK: Simon & Schuster Ltd, 1999), 282.

⁹ J. Sidlow Baxter, *Explore the Bible* (Grand Rapids, MI: Zondervan, 1987), 131.

¹⁰ Based on information from Brown, Driver, Briggs and Gesenius, "Hebrew Lexicon entry for Rea," available from http://www.biblestudytools.com/lexicons/hebrew/kjv/rea-2.html, s.v. "friend," Proverbs 17:17.

¹¹ Ibid.

¹² Psalm 121:3–4.

¹³ 3Genesis 22: 2.

¹⁴ Genesis 37:3.

¹⁵ Dr. Kevin Leman, *What a Difference a Daddy Makes* (Nashville, TN: Thomas Nelson Publishers, 2000), 22.

Endnotes

[16] 1 Corinthians 13:4 MSG.

[17] Dr. Kevin Leman, 22.

[18] Proverbs 3:13-16.

[19] Sidney Poitier, *The Measure of Man* (San Francisco, CA: Harper, 2000), taken from the front dust cover of the book.

[20] Ibid., 67.

[21] Philip Yancey, "The Crayon Man," *Christianity Today* magazine, February 1987 issue.

[22] Ibid.

[23] James 1:17 MSG.

[24] Psalm 55:14 MSG.

[25] James Robison, *My Father's Face* (Sisters, OR: Questar Publishers, Inc., 1997), 86-87.

[26] Matthew 7:11; Luke 21:1-4.

[27] Gary Chapman, *The Five Love Languages of Children*, (Chicago, IL: Northfield Publishing, 1997).

[28] Psalm 55:13–14.

[29] 2 Samuel 16:23.

[30] Psalm 55:21.

[31] Proverbs 27:6.

[32] Proverbs 27:9.

[33] Proverbs 27:14 MSG.

[34] Proverbs 15:23 MSG.

[35] Michael Ray King, "Fathers, Encourage Your Children," available from ezinearticles.com.

[36] Proverbs 18:20–21 MSG.

[37] Proverbs 18:21 .

[38] H. A. Dorfman, *Coaching the Mental Game* (Lanham, MD: Taylor Trade, 2005), 52.

[39] Ruth 1:16.

[40] 1 Samuel 18:1.

[41] Proverbs 27:10 AMP.

[42] Judges 14:20.

[43] See Exodus 33:11.

[44] See Deuteronomy 13:6; Judges 7:13–14.

[45] Job 6:14,27.

[46] Psalm 55:14, 21; thought to be David speaking of his close friend Ahitophel.

[47] Song of Solomon 5:16.

[48] Exodus 11:2.

[49] "Somebody Special," author unknown, available from http://www.mensstuff.org/issues/byissue/fathersstories.html.

Chapter 7

[1] Patrick Henry Huges, Patrick John Hughes, and Bryant Stamford, *I Am Potential* (Cambridge, MA: Da Capo Press, 2009), 52–53.

[2] Michael Q. Pink, "A Blind Man Gives Vision," June 9, 2008; available from http://www.sellingamongwolves.com/blog/2008/06/09/a-blind-man-gives-vision-a-must-see-video/.

[3] Based on information from *Learning to Dance in the Rain*, by Mac Anderson and BJ Gallagher (Naperville, IL: Simple Truths, 2008), 8.

[4] Leonard Sweet, *Summoned to Lead* (Grand Rapids, MI: Zondervan, 2004), 64–65.

[5] C. S. Lewis, *The Magician's Nephew* (New York, NY: Harper Collins, 2003), 65.

[6] Leonard Sweet, "Join the Everlasting Song," Sweet's Soul Café, 1998, Volume 3, Number 7-8-9; available from www.leonardsweet.com, 10,14.

[7] "Rescue the Perishing," words by Fanny Crosby, 1869; music by W. Howard Doane.

[8] Joachim-Ernest Berendt, *The World Is Sound: Nada Brahma: Music and the Landscape of Consciousness* (Rochester, NY: Destiny Books, 1987), 10.

[9] Luke 19:37–40.

[10] "This Is My Father's World," words by Maltbie D. Babcock, 1901.

[11] Leonard Sweet, 11.

[12] Psalm 102:25; Job 38:7 KJV.

[13] Romans 8:19 ESV.

[14] Ephesians 1:10 ESV

[15] Matthew 11:16–17.

[16] Roger Day wrote this as a personal favor to me. His professional Web address is www.therapyinromania.org.uk.

[17] Ibid.

[18] Vanessa Nowitzky, "Inner Song," available from www.singdancing.com/innersong.htm.

[19] Robert Dex, "Orphan birds given singing lessons," June 15, 2008, available from http://www.metro.co.uk/news/176717-orphan-birds-given-singing-lessons.

20 Michael Gurian, *The Purpose of Boys* (San Francisco, CA: Jossey Bass, 2009), 28.

21 Ibid., 13.

22 Ibid., 105–108.

23 2 Timothy 3:16.

24 See 2 Peter 1:21.

25 Hebrews 12:11.

Chapter 8

1 Akhil Shahani, "Business: Michael Jordan, the failure?" article available from http://www.famous-quotes-and-quotations.com/sports-quotes.html.

2 Based on information from "Five Tips for Dealing with Negative Feedback at Work" by Jill Frank, available from www.leverageyourtalent.com/negative_feedback.htm.

3 Ibid.

4 "The Pursuit of Happiness: Gardner's Climb to the Top," an article available from http://www.evancarmichael.com/Famous-Entrepreneurs/815/The-Pursuit-of-Happiness-Gardners-Climb-to-the-Top.html.

5 Rob Parsons, *Bringing Home the Prodigals* (London, England: Hodder & Stoughten, 2003), 44–45.

6 Romans 12:1–2.

7 Philippians 3:13.

8 Jeremiah 31:34; Isaiah 43:25.

9 Philippians 4:8.

10 Romans 6:11.

11 C. S. Lewis, *The Screwtape Letters*, 11th Edition (New York, NY: Macmillan Company, 1969), 68.

12 Based on information available from http://dictionary1.classic.reference.com/help/faq/language/d42.html.

13 Rob Parsons, 42–43.

14 Psalm 51:3.

15 Kent Nerburn, *Letters to My Son* (Novato, CA: New World Library, 1999), 173.

16 1 Corinthians 15:10.

17 "*A lamb for a house,*" Exodus 12:3 KJV; John 4:53; Acts 11:14; 16:15, 31, 34.

18 Excerpt from a letter by Bill Cosby, who is a supporter of the National Rally of Responsible Fatherhood 2009; available from http://www.fathersdayrally.com/rallyendorsements.html.

Chapter 9

1 John Humphreys, *Devil's Advocate* (United Kingdom: Hutchinson, 1999), 144.

2 George Bernard Shaw at Brighton, 1907, available from www.shawchicago.org/shawbio.html.

3 James C. Collins and Jerry I. Porras, *Built to Last* (New York, NY: Random House, 1994, 1997).

4 Ibid., 22.

5 *Fathers of Influence*, 76–77.

6 All of scripture is working towards a "Cosmic Conclusion" in which Jesus Christ will return to this earth and establish His kingdom, as heaven has all ways intended it to be.

7 1 Chronicles 12:32 DARBY.

8 Matthew 5:13–14.

9 Amos 3:7; 2 Timothy 3:16.

10 This description of the master/slave clock is available from http://en.wikipedia.org/wiki/Slave_clocks.

11 Ephesians 6:4 MSG.

12 Thayer and Smith, "Greek Lexicon entry for Chronos," available from http://www.studylight.org/lex/grk/view.cgi?number=5550.

13 Ibid., "Greek Lexicon entry for Kairos, available from http://www.studylight.org/lex/grk/view.cgi?number=2540.

14 Guy Chevreau, *Catch the Fire: The Toronto Blessing* (New York, NY: HarperCollins, 1995), 49.

15 Ecclesiastes 3:1.

16 John 2:4.

17 Steve Farrar, *King Me: What Every Son Wants and Needs From His Father* (Chicago, IL: Moody Publishers, 2005), 11–12.

18 Many books and Web sites on fatherhood consider dads spending time with their children to be a big issue. One such Web site this kind of information is available from is http//www.fathers.com.

19 Sermon notes written by my mom before she passed away at age 57. Also, see James 4:14.

Endnotes

Chapter 10

[1] Rick Reilly, "Strongest Dad in the World," *Sports Illustrated* magazine, June 20, 2005 issue, available from http://sportsillustrated.cnn.com/vault/article/magazine/MAG1111767/.

[2] Based on information from http://www.teamhoyt.com/about/racing-history.html.

[3] Rick Reilly, available from http://sportsillustrated.cnn.com/vault/article/magazine/MAG1111767/.

[4] *The Oxford Compact Dictionary*, University Press, 1996, s.v. "champion."

[5] James 1:2-3 PHILLIPS.

[6] 1 Timothy 6:12; Hebrews 12:1.

[7] Luke 7:11–17.

[8] Matthew 15:22–28.

[9] Luke 15:11–32.

[10] 1 Samuel 17:34–35; Numbers 16:41–50.

[11] 1 Samuel 30:1–9,16–19.

[12] Hebrews 4:16; Ephesians 6; John 10:10.

[13] Job 5:6–7 MSG.

[14] 1 Samuel 17.

[15] 1 Timothy 6:12.

[16] Romans 7:13–25; 1 Corinthians 2:6–16; Ephesians 4:17–24.

[17] Michael S. Heiser, "Clash of the Manuscripts: Goliath & the Hebrew Text of the Old Testament," *Bible Study Magazine*, available from http://www.biblestudymagazine.com/interactive/goliath.

[18] Acts 13:22.

[19] Ephesians 3:16.

[20] Based on information from Brown, Driver, Briggs and Gesenius, "Hebrew Lexicon entry for Benayim," available from http://www.biblestudytools.com/lexicons/hebrew/kjv/benayim.html, Strong's #1143, s.v. "champion," 1 Samuel 17:4,23.

[21] Ezekiel 22:30 NASB.

[22] Luke 15:11–32.

[23] Dennis Conner, *Comeback: My Race for the America's Cup* (London, England: Bloomsbury, 1987).

Chapter 11

[1] Taken from the tract *Why Good Men Fail as Fathers*, American Tract Society, available from http://www.atsdirect.org/epages/atsdirect.sf/4b74447b0a24ecb72717ac100357067d/Product/View/42218.

[2] 1 Samuel 3:13.

[3] 1 Samuel 2:23–25.

[4] 1 Samuel 4:15–18.

[5] Stephen R. Covey, *First Things First* (New York: Simon & Schuster Ltd, 1994), 44.

[6] Brown, Driver, Briggs and Gesenius, "Hebrew Lexicon entry for Sar," available from http://www.biblestudytools.com/lexicons/hebrew/kjv/sar.html, Strong's #8269, s.v. "captain."

[7] Joshua 5:14 KJV.

[8] Genesis 2:15 MSG.

[9] See Matthew 8:5–13.

[10] Romans 5:17.

[11] Proverbs 3:5.

[12] 1 Corinthians 15:10.

[13] Romans 5:17.

[14] Not the person's real name.

[15] Not the person's real name.

[16] 2 Timothy 4:7.

[17] Ecclesiastes 3:11.

[18] Romans 2:6.

[19] Based on information from *Wiktionary*, available from http://en.wiktionary.org/wiki/seize_the_day, s.v. "Carpe Diem."

[20] Rick Weinberg, *Derek and dad finish Olympic 400 together*, special to ESPN.com, available from http://sports.espn.go.com/espn/espn25/story?page=moments/94.

[21] Hebrews 12:1 MSG.

[22] 2 Timothy 4:7.

[23] 1 Corinthians 15:10.

Made in the USA
Charleston, SC
28 October 2010